Actions of Play

Actions of Play

Weaving Play Schemas into Inquiry-Based Learning and Project Work

Lisa Agogliati and Heather Jackson

Foreword by Susan Stacey

Redleaf Press®
www.redleafpress.org
800-423-8309

Published by Redleaf Press
10 Yorkton Court
St. Paul, MN 55117
www.redleafpress.org

First edition 2025
Cover design by Michelle Lee Lagerroos
Cover photographs by the authors
Interior design by Michelle Lee Lagerroos
Typeset in Ezigio URW, Futura PT, and Duper
Interior photos by Lisa Agogliati, Heather Jackson, Julie Hunter, Ashley Nartey, Hitomi Inoue, Kelsey O'Brien, Laura Sheedy, Katie Deane Brophy, and Sophie Chambers
Printed in the United States of America
32 31 30 29 28 27 26 25   1 2 3 4 5 6 7 8

Library of Congress Cataloging-in-Publication Data
Names: Agogliati, Lisa, 1967- author. | Jackson, Heather, 1959- author.
Title: Actions of play : weaving play schemas into inquiry-based learning and project work / by Lisa Agogliati and Heather Jackson.
Description: First edition. | St. Paul, MN : Redleaf Press, 2025. | Includes bibliographical references and index. | Summary: "This book builds on recent research and revelations about play schemas to transform understanding of play-based learning and project work in early childhood programs. Play schemas are the patterns of actions that play takes-transporting, enclosing, rotating, and more-the verbs of play rather than the nouns. The repetitive behaviors, play patterns, and play intentions of schemas facilitate children's brain development and also help them make sense of their world"— Provided by publisher.
Identifiers: LCCN 2024036667 (print) | LCCN 2024036668 (ebook) | ISBN 9781605548272 (paperback) | ISBN 9781605548289 (ebook)
Subjects: LCSH: Play. | Child development. | Early childhood education--Activity programs.
Classification: LCC LB1139.35.P55 A46 2025 (print) | LCC LB1139.35.P55 (ebook) | DDC 372.21--dc23/eng/20240821
LC record available at https://lccn.loc.gov/2024036667
LC ebook record available at https://lccn.loc.gov/2024036668

Printed on acid-free paper

Lisa

To Tim, Tessa, and my family

For the children at NCRC, especially the Explorers, who taught me how "wondering often leads to something wonderful." (From *Dragonboy* by Fabio Napoleoni)

Heather

Dedication means a feeling of very strong support for or loyalty to someone or something. I dedicate this book to the educators I have worked with at the Sunflower School over the past fifteen years who have inspired me with their work and led me to want something more than traditional early childhood education.

I also dedicate this book to my daughters, Sarah and Rachel, and sister, Kathleen, whom I work with every day at the Sunflower School. Without their support, I could not do all the amazing side projects I have going on. And finally, to my husband, who makes dinner for me every night and understands the importance of my work and lovingly supports me.

Contents

Foreword

In early years education, we tend to be great observers of children. When we value their play as learning, we notice, take notes, reflect, and make decisions based on what we've seen. This cycle is at the core of inquiry-based programs and emergent curricula. For many of us, this is our way of being in the classroom and co-constructing with young children.

As we all know, the early years classroom is a tremendously busy one. Children are playing, talking, building, exploring, and negotiating. They have big ideas and sometimes unusual strategies. It is delightfully messy and nonlinear. And the educators in the room are trying to make meaning of what they are seeing and hearing. It is a complex process that Lisa Agogliati and Heather Jackson help us to navigate *Actions of Play: Weaving Schemas into Inquiry-Based Learning and Project Work.*

How do we identify what we are seeing in children's patterns of movement and repetitive play—the basis of what we call *schemas*? And just as important, how do we actually use that which we have named within our play and inquiry-based programs? Lisa and Heather use their own experiences, together with their knowledge of schema theory and inquiry-based practices, to help us transform our practice from the simplicity of simple themes, to the wonderful complexity of inquiries that all children thrive upon.

Within this book, we find a way to use verbs rather than nouns. For instance, the example of *rainbow* (a noun) is used; yet rather than this noun, which is limiting, we might think of a rainbow as the *transforming* of colors within the sky, which gives us much more scope and possibility for exploration. Using practical and easy-to-understand examples, together with reflective questions to ponder with one's team, Lisa and Heather suggest new ways to develop your program that move us away from prescribed and published curricula.

We are reminded, through their writing, that it is not our job to answer questions for children, but rather to provide the means for discovery; to be a co-constructor of learning. Whether this is through an inquiry, a project, or small moments within our days with children, when we recognize schema and incorporate them into our existing practices, we have a basket of possibilities to consider—a broadening of our thinking, or as the authors describe it, a "play tapestry" of action-based construction of knowledge.

A tapestry is an apt description for Lisa and Heather's work. The weaving of our own knowledge with that of the children, theory interwoven with practice, and intuition combined with observation, leads us to a program that is intentional, authentic, and responsive. There are many ways you might use this book, but at the core of Lisa and Heather's suggestions is a deep respect for children and a sensitive gaze upon their work.

—Susan Stacey

Acknowledgments

Lisa

My life changed significantly in 2009 as I began a new chapter of teaching at the National Child Research Center (NCRC) and was introduced to the art of emergent curriculum under the exceptional leadership of Liz Barclay and Tiffany Williams. At NCRC I felt like a kid in a candy shop, constantly in awe of the journey of learning that emerged from my colleagues and the children year after year. It was the unexpected situation of teaching during COVID, however, that gave me an opportunity to slow down, listen, and challenge myself to grow as an educator in ways I had never imagined as I began learning about and working with play schemas. After I shared my profound experiences with former head of school Val Wise, she immediately urged me to document what had inadvertently become a year of action research. With her incredible support and guidance, I took the time to capture the results of my work over the past three years. As I continued my research at NCRC, I have been fortunate to receive tremendous support from the administration, including Molli Anderson, James Carroll, and Francesca Gallozzi, along with the NCRC community, board of trustees, and parents.

This book would not have been possible without the time and talents of my colleagues, especially Julie Hunter and Ashley Nartey, whose expertise in the fields of nature and diversity were pivotal in creating a framework and supplying resources for using play schemas for our faculty—and now for educators beyond the doors of our school in Washington, DC. My heartfelt thanks go out to the talented and dedicated current and former NCRC faculty who have shared their reflections on schema and curriculum: Hitomi Inoue, Kelsey O'Brien, Carolee Clay, Sarah Chatzkel, Katie Deane Brophy, Laura Sheedy, Hannah Schaefer, and Tarah Leroy. Special thanks to Resource Teachers Sophie Chambers and Jennifer McMahon for their work with Explorer students in 2020–2021 and for their support of my initial foray into building investigations with and around play schemas. I would also like to thank NCRC's faculty for their work exploring schema in their curriculum and for being so supportive of this project. In addition, I was extremely fortunate to collaborate with veteran educators working in the public school system with published early childhood curricula, including Janine Levin and Emily Paterson at Maury Elementary School, Washington, DC, and Dr. Tamanika Odinga and Stephanie Dunmiles at the Early Childhood Community Network in St. Charles Parish Public Schools, Louisiana.

Since becoming NCRC's pedagogista, I have been incredibly grateful to receive personal mentorship from author Susan Stacey and to learn from her about best practices in emergent curriculum. None of this work could be possible without our talented editor Melissa York, whose guidance at every step of this process has been invaluable. Above all, I wish to thank my new colleague and friend, Heather Jackson, for sharing her vision of writing a book for educators with me. I have learned a great deal from her and am thankful for the opportunity to collaborate with such a talented educator, and I have enjoyed much laughter and joy along our journey.

Heather

I want to acknowledge and thank the many children I have worked with over the years. My research is about them and their astonishing work. Children deserve an important and interesting early childhood experience so that they can feel confident in expressing their ideas. I believe that without Reggio-inspired practice, my career would have been marginal. My heart has been filled with joy as I've worked through so many theories that I've read about in following this approach. Over the past twenty years, I've been on this amazing journey with children, and it has opened my mind to their ways of thinking in ways that I never could have imagined on my own. Three years ago, I implemented a new half-day program within our school called Makerspace, which was inspired by the book *Makerspaces: Remaking Your Play and STEAM Early Learning Areas* by Michelle Kay Compton and Robin Chappele Thompson (Redleaf Press 2020). This experience of working back in the classroom has given me hands-on, real-life project work experience. At the Sunflower School, I work with fellow educator Danica, whom I have known for thirteen years. Our practice encompasses play schemas, which give us so many *aha* moments in our days with children. Thank you to the children who show magical thinking, try new materials with enthusiasm and joy, and pursue their never-ending curiosity about their world.

I also want to thank Lisa, my coauthor. We had never met, and Redleaf brought us together. I was amazed by how many of our work experiences were so similar and how our work in play schemas has profoundly affected us. We have had many online meetings and conversations about how we were feeling about the book-writing process. Writing a book can be overwhelming and daunting, but Lisa somehow understood my worries and apprehension even over Zoom. After each of our discussions, I was refreshed and ready to continue—and thank goodness, because otherwise I would not be here writing these words.

Introduction

Drawn by Heather Jackson, 2024

Weaving involves crossing two threads, the warp and the weft, one vertical and the other horizontal, one stretched taut and the other undulating and intertwined with the first. To produce the textile it is necessary for these two threads to be bound, otherwise each will remain a fragile and fluttering potentiality. . . . If the meeting of opposites does not take place, nothing is created, for each element is defined by its opposite and takes its meaning from it.

—Dario Valcarenghi, *Kilim: History and Symbols*

This book is about the weaving together of two early childhood educators' ideas, theories, and stories about play schemas and how they have influenced our work with children. The quote above strikes us as an important part of our play schema work and our work as educators. We have interwoven and entangled our discussions and conversations over our year of writing to create a beautiful tapestry of work that we hope will intrigue you so you notice something deeper in the play of children.

Play puts us into a powerful flow, and we become absorbed in the joy of the moment. When we are participating in something joyful, our minds are open to creativity and learning. Children value play for the joyful experience it is. We as adults sometimes see play as something to do to keep busy. Our adult gaze should see play as the work of children, something of the utmost importance. We see children playing the same way repeatedly. They're trying to make meaning of their world, and play allows them to do this. These repeated actions, which we can call play schemas, allow us as adults to see into the mind of a child. Play schemas guide us to the purpose of children's play.

Educator Sally Haughey once posed the question, "What if everyone already knew the word 'play' was synonymous with the word 'education'?" She went on to muse, "Imagine how the typical learning environment would look, sound, and feel if we considered these two words interchangeable, so that one wasn't considered 'frivolous' while the other was considered essential to a child's development?" Our commitment as educators to recognize the essential role of play in developing children's cognitive and social-emotional skills can result in educational experiences where children, as Haughey put it, "emerge as confident learners with the skills that will make them active participants in a future world that works for a diverse and changing population" (2021).

Dr. Laura A. Jana notes in her TEDx Talk *Skills Every Child Will Need to Succeed in 21st Century* that a vital piece to children's development in these early years is "making sure they continue to see the world around them as a question mark" (2018). The essence of play is to *engage* in something that depends on physical action. If we return to the image of the loom, the warp (vertical threads) can represent children's play across their entire day. The resulting pattern or design depends on the weft (horizontal threads), which could represent materials, time, type of environment (inside versus outside), small-group gatherings, or children's wondering questions. The essential tool to combine the weft with the warp is the shuttle, which moves the weft threads back and forth across the loom. As early childhood educators, we move through the cycle of observing, listening, reflecting (as teachers and with the children), and responding. This is the delicate movement of the shuttle as we carry out intentional conversations and invitations to support our observations of the children's actions and ultimately their inquiry.

When we look deeper into this joy of action woven together with the learning environment, the nature of the play comes into focus as specific patterns of movement—schemas.

Heather's Initial Experiences with Play Schemas

Play schemas are defined as repetitive behaviors, play patterns, and play intentions that children demonstrate through play and that facilitate development of the brain. Play schemas have several categories, including *connection/disconnection, transforming, trajectory, transporting, orientation, positioning, rotation, enveloping,* and *enclosing.*

Play schemas are at the heart and soul of my work with young children. I am the executive director of the Sunflower School in Orangeville, Ontario, and my practice has been inspired by the schools of Reggio Emilia in Italy since 1998. I have been fortunate to travel the world to learn about this amazing way of being with young children. I was introduced to play schemas in 2015 by a colleague, Cindy Green, who was a professor at Seneca College, Toronto, Ontario. I listened intently to the *what* and *how* of play schemas, and they truly intrigued me because I was able to see them appear in the children's play. They became a key part of my work with children.

I also did research on my own, reading *Threads of Thinking: Schemas and Young Children's Learning* by Cathy Nutbrown (2011), which highlights the theory and research behind play schemas. Then in 2019 I read *Children's Lively Minds: Schema Theory Made Visible* by Deb Curtis and Nadia Jaboneta (2019). It led me to a fuller understanding of how play schemas are children's way of making meaning in their worlds.

Play schemas naturally led me to the concept of verbs as projects. Project work is not a weekly theme about a noun like *firefighter*. Rather, it's about really observing your children's playing and defining that play in terms of a play schema or a verb. Slow down and notice what the children are noticing. What is fascinating to the children in their play? When you record these ideas and periodically reflect on them, project work becomes research for you and the children. I had always thought that using nouns as project work—such as *community helpers* or *winter*—was very simplistic and repetitive for educators. I was fortunate to attend a session on Reggio-inspired practice with the Acorn School in Richmond Hill, Ontario, with Rosalba Bortolotti, and it was there that the idea of verbs entered the conversation. Using verbs allows us to create more complex project work than using simple nouns.

For example, instead of using the theme of *winter*, why not use the verb *transforming*, which is a play schema? How does the snow fall from the sky? How does snow turn to ice and water? How does the world transform into a cold, wintery environment? How does autumn transform into winter? These questions become a pathway into magical storytelling for the children. We can view *winter* through the lens of multiple play schemas too. The children are fascinated with the sidewalk plow and watching snow flying through the air, which brings us to questions of *transporting*. How can we transport snow? How does the snowplow transport snow? How are snowflakes transported from the sky? How might we transport snow with wind? *Enclosing* and *enveloping* also come into the children's play as they cover materials with snow on our playgrounds and create big snow hills, small enclosures,

and forts. Once we move from nouns to verbs, the simple theme of *winter* becomes complex and creative when thinking about play schemas. It should be our intention as early childhood educators to make our work complex for the children and ourselves. The value that play schemas bring to our everyday life in early childhood education is creativity, innovation, and joy.

At the Sunflower School, we are constantly searching for play schemas in our work with children. Throughout this book you will read about real-life projects and stories of the children and educators at the Sunflower School and how they view their work from a lens of play schemas and verbs. Verbs are filled with action, engagement, and thinking, and so is a child's joyful play. Joy and play must be woven together in all experiences for young children. Joyful play is a full-body experience, and so are verbs. Verbs are defined by an action, or a state of being. The theory behind joyful play says that it sparks the brain's reward centers and triggers a feel-good chemical called dopamine. Higher dopamine is linked to better memory, attention, creativity, mental flexibility, and motivation.

Lisa's Initial Experiences with Play Schemas

Although I have taught in early childhood since 1989, my first experience with emergent curriculum occurred when I started teaching at the National Child Research Center (NCRC) in 2009. When following an emergent curriculum, educators plan lessons and activities led by interests of the children. The exploration (or progression into a deeper investigation) is guided by further inquiries from the children and teachers as well as by detailed documentation of teachers' observations of the children's play, engagement with materials, and conversations.

My experiences with implementing emergent curriculum relied on team observations of what the children were creating, playing, or talking about in the classroom. The teaching team would then move forward with a series of invitations we felt would be interesting to the children. Next, we would evaluate how the interest progressed (or not) among the class. Then we would determine whether the topic was ready to be expanded into a longer investigation framed by research questions generated by the children.

Early in my work as an early childhood teacher, I was aware of schema as it relates to Jean Piaget's theory of cognitive development and the way children group their knowledge of the world around them. It wasn't until later in my career that I learned of another way of understanding schema, when I began to incorporate loose parts into the classroom. I initially thought about loose parts in terms of categories of materials, such as paper, plastic, metal, natural items, or fabric. When I discovered Michelle Thornhill's chart *Loose Parts and Intelligent Playthings Categorized by Schema,* I used the resource primarily for identifying new kinds of loose parts. As my work developed with play schema, I then used the resource to learn more about the movement of materials and how it appears in children's play.

In 2018 I discovered the work of Susan Stacey with *Emergent Curriculum in Early Childhood Settings: From Theory to Practice* (2018), which launched me into a more intentional way of using my observations of the children's play and their conversations (verbal and nonverbal). This led me to reconsider the role of researcher for both children and teachers. That same year I became our school's pedagogista to support teaching teams with resources for developing emergent curriculum. We later adopted Stacey's book as our

Scan this QR code or browse to www.brucecounty.on.ca/sites/default/files/Loose%20Parts%20By%20Schema_0.pdf to see Michelle Thornhill's chart.

curriculum anchor. It serves as part of our orientation for teachers new to our school (or new to emergent curriculum), and it offers a wealth of ideas for veteran teachers as well.

My focus in my first two years in this role (while still teaching in the classroom, as I have continued to do) was to support teams in maximizing time in their schedule for play and to encourage them to slow the pace of moving forward with (or ending) a topic of interest in their class. We experimented in working with different templates for recording observations, based on Stacey's *The Unscripted Classroom: Emergent Curriculum in Action* (2011), and for including teachers' questions in the emergent curriculum process.

We also focused on establishing a central place for documentation in each classroom, which we call Research Boards. I was motivated by a visit to a local Reggio-inspired school, where I saw in each classroom a large metal board that served as a gathering place for documentation of objects and

Explorer Research Board
FLAMINGO RESEARCH STATION
Explorer Questions:
WHERE do flamingos live?
WHERE does it find mud?
WHERE does it lay its egg -- on the side, middle, or the edge of the nest?
WHERE does the mud come from?
WHERE do they lay their nests?
HOW long is their nest?
HOW big is their nest?
WHY do they have long legs?
HOW tall is a flamingo?
WHY do they have bumps on their legs?

How does the water spray out?
How does the fountain shoot up the water?
How did they get the water to the fountain?
What machines and tools do they use to make fountains?
Japanese Garden

Waddle
How do penguins move?
Slide

paper. Afterward I put magnetic bulletin boards in each classroom at NCFC in an initiative to make current emergent curriculum investigations visible throughout the school. Each board is labeled with its class's name, and each board is styled the same so that staff, students, families, and visitors can easily recognize this intentional area for making the children's questions, discoveries, and research visible.

During the summer of 2020, I virtually attended the Boulder Journey School Summer Conference. A session presented by Kirsten Zimbelman, "Math Is . . . : Toddlers' Studies of Mathematics through Line and Trajectory," explored the relationship between math concepts and play schemas. This session broadened my understanding of schema as a way that children can approach, explore, and learn cognitive skills.

As a result of my new interest, I chose play schemas for a faculty research topic. I was eager to deepen my own observation and documentation of the children's play through this lens. I was also curious to explore the effects of incorporating the language of schema types (such as *transforming* or *transporting*) into our classroom conversations and to observe how children's schemas could inform investigations.

My invitation to faculty that fall included a query based on the Boulder Journey School session:

> What is the play [schema] telling you about what the children are trying to understand?

My initial thinking with this question was to encourage teachers to focus their observations on the children's actions as they played with materials inside the classroom as well as on their engagement with materials and playground spaces.

And then we were launched into the reality of teaching during COVID.

Preparing to teach in the 2020–2021 school year in a pandemic meant shifting from twelve years of sharing the directing teacher role with a colleague to being the sole directing teacher on our team. I was also about to depart from my usual dynamic of teaching approximately twenty four- and five-year-olds to having a small "pod" of eight prekindergartners, in accordance with our licensing protocols.

The biggest question on my mind, however, was not about COVID. It was simply, "Will I still feel like the teacher I know I am? Will I still be able to make connections with my students?" With so many guidelines to follow for every part of our day, I worried that my relationship-based teaching style would be overwhelmed by monitoring temperatures, adjusting masks, repeating frequent reminders to "Make room for each other," keeping track of who touched what, and, of course, cleaning in a never-ending cycle.

With classes and faculty restricted from commingling, isolation set in. Teachers, administrators, families, and children faced huge unknowns. Video calls provided us options to meet when possible in our busy schedules, but our faculty faced immense challenges: learning how to teach in a hybrid format (with some children attending only virtually and others in the classroom); learning how to use programs such as Zoom, Seesaw, and Epic; and spending countless hours planning, arranging the room with our new six-feet social distancing in place, and implementing many new protocols for mask wearing, contact tracing, handwashing, and disinfecting materials.

My pedagogista plans were put on pause, giving way to the reality of the weight teachers were carrying for the safety of their children and themselves. Even my own excitement to explore the use of play schema in my classroom waned, and I found myself reverting back to using my observations to identify a topic for possible investigation.

I initially thought having only eight students would mean having more time with children, making it easier to determine their interests. But I found looking for a topic for our first investigation to be much harder than any other year. During the first two weeks, I noticed the children were engaged with materials inside the classroom and loved exploring the different areas of our playground, but no topic stood out to me as a potential direction. I was starting to feel frustrated. I had done this many times before, so why couldn't I figure it out now?

Although I had recently expanded my knowledge of play schemas, I still didn't quite know how I would use them as a tool for devising curriculum. My sense was that the schemas might enhance the children's experience once I had identified an investigation topic—but that was where I seemed to be stuck. It wasn't until I felt the despair of not being able to find a topic that I went back to thinking about schemas.

As I reflected on notes, photos, and videos from our classroom, I came upon a video clip of a child playing outside with chalk, focusing on his actions as he made short marks and then moved his hand across the marks to blend them together. As I watched the clip, I realized that this ordinary moment of a child playing with chalk was a true learning encounter because he was slowing down and being present. At one point, the child looked at me and commented, "So, I'm making this." We then began a simple conversation about what he was making, and I found myself intentionally using different references to the action of *transforming*:

Lisa: *When does it have the transforming part?*

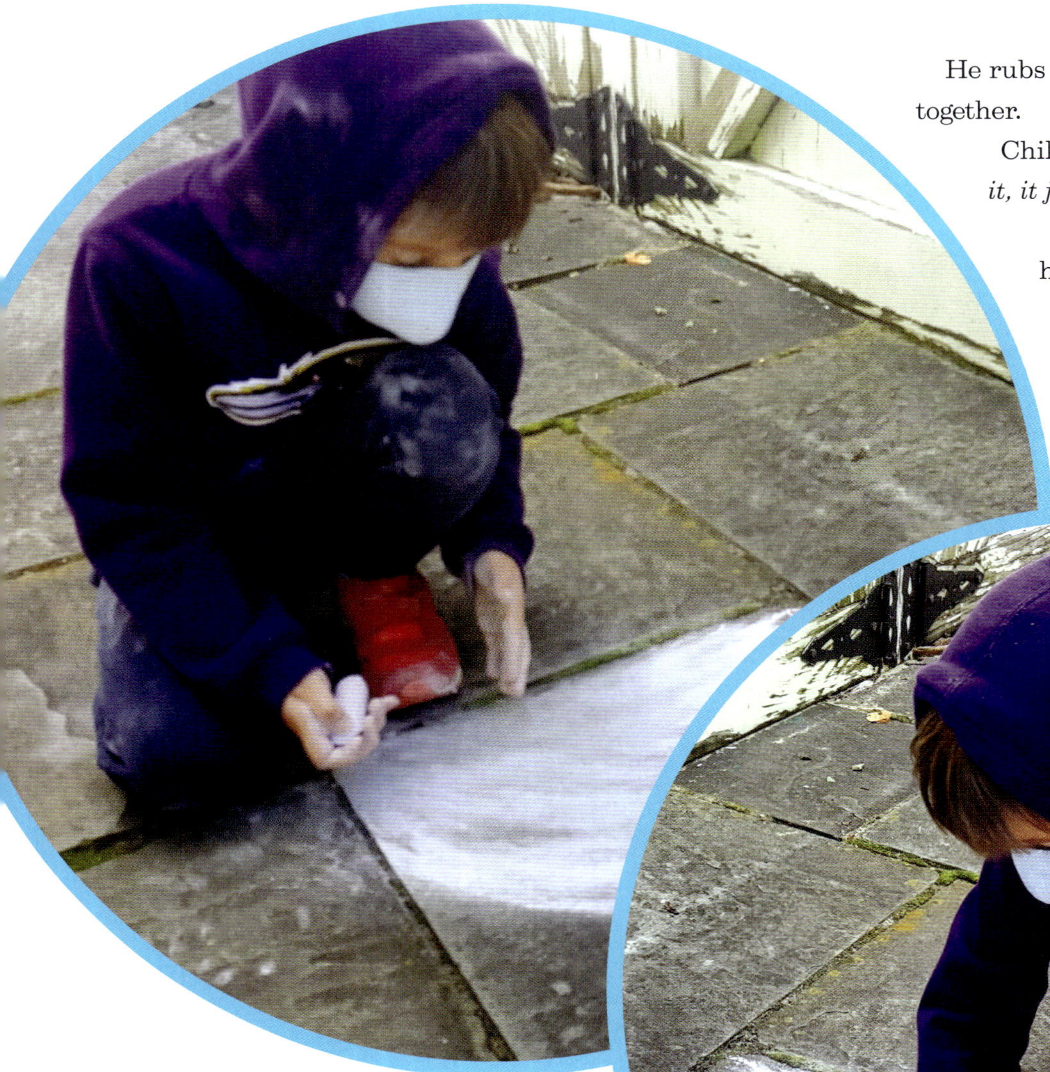

He rubs the marks to blend together.

Child: *Now. Whenever I rub it, it just . . .*

He pauses to show me his discovery again as he makes a new mark and then rubs it.

Lisa: *It changes, doesn't it?*

Child: *Yeah, I know. From my hand . . . and I don't know why. My hand is not magical but I'm just rubbing it and . . . just makes it like this.*

I continue to describe my observations of his actions.

Lisa: It's interesting because you move your hand to change the chalk. If you just touch what you drew [he taps his hand on the lines he had just drawn], *nothing changes.*

Our conversation allowed me to understand the child's thinking, gain a sense of his interests, observe his curious disposition, and witness his emotional engagement. This learning encounter became a catalyst to sharpen my observations of the children's play going forward and to home in on the movement of materials. I discovered that the schema *was* the topic evident in the children's play and their interests, which ultimately led to a lengthy investigation centered on *transforming*. This was a view into play schemas like I had never experienced before.

Even after my many years in the field of early childhood, that year stood out as one of my most significant periods of growth as a teacher. As the world managed a horrendous virus and we all navigated the loss of life's routines, I discovered this gem of play schema. It not only kept me going but also drove me to a point where I could not contain all the experiences myself—which ultimately led me to writing this book.

In the second half of that year, I continued to connect (virtually) with our teaching teams through regular meetings, and I slowly introduced information about play schemas to build up faculty's knowledge of this theory so they could begin to identify these components within their children's play. Indeed, something had clearly changed for me that fall semester, with my personal risk-taking in using a schema rather than a specific topic to drive an investigation. My view of schemas had drastically expanded beyond understanding them in conjunction with open-ended materials to now utilizing the *action* of the schemas themselves to launch possible avenues of learning. I felt a deep commitment to document the rich stories from the children who were integral to my journey as well as to document the faculty's work with observing and responding to children's play schemas.

At the end of the school year, I began to research more about the intriguing (and ultimately symbiotic) relationship between play schemas and investigations in emergent curriculum settings. I also pursued research on ways to expand play schemas into a "lens" for exploring the arts, nature/science, and our community. For this research, I received help from NCRC's director of diversity, equity, and inclusion and from a veteran teacher who worked with faculty on incorporating nature into their investigations and created resources for learning about nature.

My documentation of the relationships between play schemas and emergent curriculum investigations ultimately became the catalyst for my journey in sharing this approach with the wider early childhood community. Since that formative year teaching in my little "pod" of eight students, I have continued to witness the value of play schema–inspired investigations, especially their impact on children's ability to engage in a deeper level of exploration and, ultimately, their own inquiry.

The Why of This Book

While our journeys to applying play schemas to emergent curriculum investigations and project work were different, our foundational step in discovering the power of play schemas is the same. We both first spent time gaining an understanding of this natural tool young children are wired to use in their everyday, ever-evolving exploration of the world around them. In their seminal work *Children's Lively Minds*, authors Deb Curtis and Nadia Jaboneta (2019) present schema theory in a scaffolded format that moves educators from building their own schema vocabulary around the eight most common areas to understanding its relationship to children's social-emotional learning and brain development. Curtis and Jaboneta then expand on using the concept of schema as a tool for building math skills, exploring literacy, enhancing art experiences, and crafting advance play scripts for imagination play.

In each child's experience with play schemas, movement is at the core. The materials they engage with allow them to move through the actions of different schemas throughout their play, such as *transporting, transforming*, and *trajectory*. For educators who are interested in using schemas as either a driving force for or a transition tool with curriculum, it is critical to thoroughly understand the characteristics of the individual play schemas, which then inform their observations and reflections. Equally important is the type of materials offered, which should include a range of size and sensory elements that deepen the children's schema explorations (Curtis and Jaboneta 2019). A vital component to our process of project work and investigations is establishing a strong thread of small- and whole-group dialogues with children. We also both incorporate loose parts as a regular tool for gathering research questions with the children as it relates to the schemas they are exploring.

As we, Heather and Lisa, each gained traction in our work with identifying play schemas and expanding our observations of the children's play to include schemas, we found ourselves with a similar line of inquiry: "Where does our work with schema go from here?" For Lisa, it was a question of "How do we move further into play schemas beyond materials?" and "How could schema help with creating and implementing emergent curriculum?" Heather asked, "How might we build a curriculum using verbs instead of nouns?" and "How might we interweave our children's play with play schemas and create projects?"

The results of our subsequent connection as coauthors (and new colleagues) culminated in an opportunity to share our action research findings with early childhood educators—this book. Even as veteran teachers, we both feel that our shift to intentionally work with play schema to implement emergent curriculum and project work transformed us as educators.

How to Use This Book

We envision this book as a resource for educators who wish to further expand their work with play schemas through a weaving of rich action language and who wish to use the lens of schema to launch investigations/project work in early childhood. This approach to working with young children is driven, literally and figuratively, by the actions of their play and the investigation of that intrinsic movement of play schema as it relates to the world around them. As we document the children's inquiries as well as our own, we see patterns of *connecting*, *layering*, and *trajectory* ideas.

For educators new to working with schema theory, this book offers a format to learn how to apply schemas observed in the classroom to common learning topics in early childhood education—the study of self-expression/art, nature/science, and discovering connections to their community/world. For educators already familiar with schema theory and creating invitations for their students in support of schemas observed in their play, this book offers ideas for further fusing schema play into the curriculum (whether emergent or some other specific framework), especially as a tool to identify potential project work.

In chapter 1, we consider how following children's intentions can develop into observing the actions of a child's play through the lens of a verb instead of a noun. How do we observe the play in action, a verb, and create interesting and important research projects to document? Early childhood education is about engaging, making, constructing, building, and, most importantly, thinking. These verbs form the basis of the research in this chapter.

Chapter 2 explores how we might apply play schemas to deepen children's learning experiences even while using different types of curricula. Following discussion of setting up an environment that fosters schema play and using "juicy verbs" to describe children's play, the chapter considers how to apply schema while adhering to various published curricula, and it also draws connections with children's literature and social-emotional learning.

In chapter 3, we consider how the basic questions we ask children have a different intention than the questions we use to further play-based learning or to do action research. As educators, we need to rethink theme-based learning and start to generate research projects in our work with young children, even toddlers. These questions will be used to create invitations, provocations, and play proposals that the children answer in their play.

Chapter 4 shares Lisa's extended stories from NCRC about her experiences using schemas as the basis for emergent curriculum, and linking the schemas across investigations of art, nature, and connections with community and the world.

Similarly, chapter 5 includes Heather's stories from the Sunflower School, showing how the educators highlight verbs and play schemas with each project.

The conclusion documents our reflections and discoveries from our collaboration and offers final words and suggestions. The appendices offer copious suggested resources to support the implementation and documentation of play schemas with young children.

Our hope is for readers to reimagine their inquiry-based learning work by using play schemas to create complex and rich experiences for young children and educators.

CHAPTER 1

Discovering the Verb in the Noun

HEATHER JACKSON

Play is our brain's favorite way of learning
—Diane Ackerman

I want to challenge the way we usually think about following children's interests in our work as early childhood educators. Children's play is complex and very intentional. There is a prevailing understanding that play-based learning is a "free-for-all" and that teachers lose control of the work, but this is not so.

When we observe, we see that children's intentions are rich in play schemas and verbs as projects. As educators, we help guide the play by incorporating verbs into our work and by using our knowledge of play schemas, Reggio-inspired principles, and Loris Malaguzzi's one hundred languages of children. When we think deeply about children's play, we will see that it is the children's intentions we need to pay attention to rather than the simplistic interests.

According to Webster's dictionary, an *interest* is a passive idea or topic. Yet children's ideas are not passive. Their play is dynamic, full-bodied, and engaging. An *intention* is an aim or a plan, a purpose, intent, objective, goal, target, design, play schema, idea, wish, or dream. Having researched the meanings of both words, I have become even more convinced that children's play is based on *intentions*, which are more powerful and complex than a simple, passive *interest*. Intentions show us children's relationships with their imaginations and their creativity, which drive their learning and exploration of the world.

Using Children's Intentions to Build Complexity

Children need complexity, which helps build their brains and their understanding of the world. Often, early childhood is filled with simplistic ways of being because we feel toddlers and preschoolers are not capable and competent. We *say* they are capable and competent, but many times our programs don't realize it. Rather, how can we build complexity into our project work with young children by using their intentions?

Physically, you can see this idea of complexity when children are learning to use scissors. The simple way for children to learn is by using childproof safety scissors. The complex way is to start with proper scissors and cutting in a hundred different ways. In *Art and Creativity in Reggio Emilia*, Vea Vecchi from Reggio Children says that "learning to use tools like scissors is not a simple task of learning how to hold and then cut, but rather learning how to use scissors to cut is to build a child's relationship with materials like paper" (Vecchi 2010). We believe that children need a hundred different experiences with the tools in our classroom to learn how to use them and then in turn create relationships with materials.

Using scissors is an everyday opportunity for the children in our classroom. We have a small table set up for two children to practice and master the use of scissors. We have observed that the children help each other hold the scissors and teach each other to cut the paper. They are very aware of being safe with the scissors, and they will alert a teacher when someone is not safe.

As educators, we also build complexity by investigating and observing the intentions of the children during play. Intentions are another way to label play schemas. Play schemas include *transporting* materials or themselves (flying is a magical preschool dream), *transforming* (turning mud into cakes), *enveloping* (making materials disappear), and *enclosing* (building forts inside and outside), as well as *positioning*, *orientation*, and *rotation* (moving materials around in the world).

The words *wish* and *dream* in my dictionary's definition of *intention* caught my imagination and attention as powerful intentions of children. They wish and dream every day in their play and use their imagination to fully realize what they are trying to figure out in the world. Children don't have filters as adults do, so fairies do exist for them, and even scary monsters are real and vivid. As educators, we build on their imaginations of wishes and dreams to create beautiful early childhood experiences, and play schemas and intentions are the lens with which we do that.

What are children's dreams? I love that we can think about what the children are dreaming for. This is a big idea in our work. As I write this, I know that the preschoolers in my program right now wish to catch a star in the sky. This work has been ongoing for two months. The verb for our project is *wishing*, and this word can carry us all year long. This excites my imagination, and it brings many possibilities for our work. In their hearts and imaginations, the children believe they can catch a star, and it is my job as the educator to help them fully realize it. We like to make word webs and charts to explore our ideas, like the web here that we made to talk about catching a star.

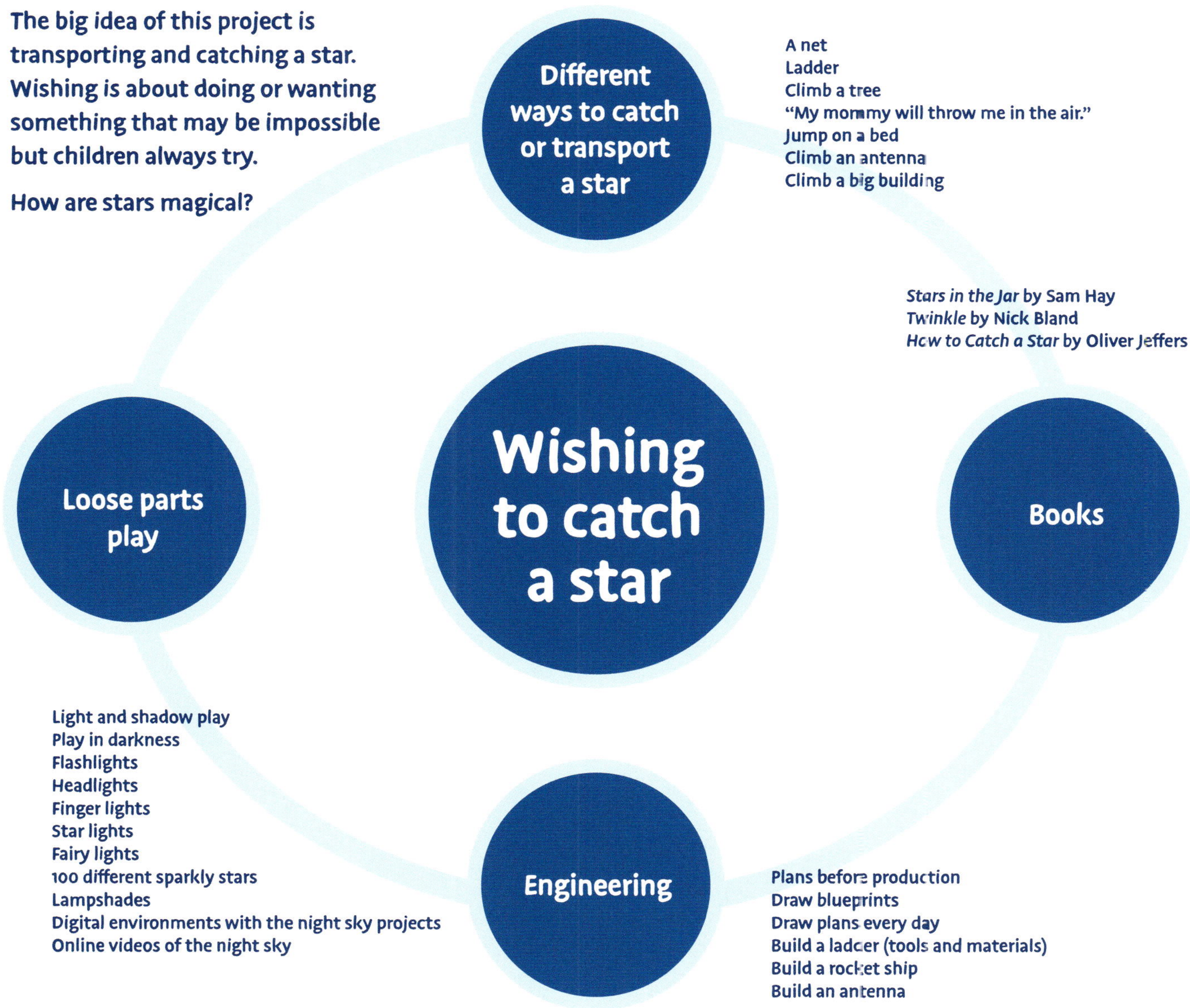

How can we help children fully realize their dreams and wishes through play schemas and intentions? What are our intentions as educators? What is our wish or dream for project work? These questions are powerful and bring both magic and thoughtfulness to our work.

Take a minute to think about a wish or dream you have right now for your work. Write it down in your journal, and revisit it often. Your wish or dream will have more meaning when you write it down. Each project should have a wish or a dream from the children's points of view, the educators' points of view, and the families' points of view.

The intentions of the teachers must emerge along with the intentions of the children. Our questions and wonders generate curiosity about the children's play. As teacher-researchers, our ideas are important in the work of our children.

We all know that if we see a child jumping off a rock or tree stump and ask them, "How can you fly?" magical answers and imaginative theories will burst forth. Most three-year-olds believe they can jump and fly—therefore, from this work comes a project about flying. *Flying* is the verb, and it begets a complex idea. To a child, flying is magical. Fairies fly, airplanes fly, and ladybugs fly, so why can't they fly? It is not my intention to tell them they can't fly but rather to give them the tools, words, and experiences to see if maybe they could fly.

We can witness the power of the children's thinking as they explain how flying can happen. And if we are fully present and respectful of their magical thinking, then we can imagine ways to help them fly by creating wings, drawing blueprints of wings, researching different types of wings, watching YouTube videos of people flying gliders or early airplanes, and looking at Leonardo da Vinci's blueprints of wings.

Educators must learn when it is best to ask questions. We could videotape that child jumping off the rock and then play it back and ask what they were thinking when they were jumping: "Did you believe you could fly? How does the wind help us fly?" The questions in my mind as an educator are abundant, but I need to tune in to the children's intentions surrounding this flying play and focus my questions on what they are trying to figure out. As an educator in this project, I ask myself, "Is the point actually figuring out how to fly?" Probably not—the real work is not in understanding aerodynamics but in the child's exploration of flying and drawing of flying, and the act of researching with children and making meaning. The latter is one of the most important elements of this work: the children are trying to figure out, to make meaning of flying.

I learned from studying Vygotsky that "a child's play is not simply a reproduction of what he has experienced but a creative reworking of the impressions he has acquired" (1976). This is what I believe are the child's intentions during play.

For example, one child's family is having a baby. The child talks about this baby that is coming, but they are not sure how and when. They are watching as their mother's tummy gets bigger and bigger, and there is talk about doctor appointments and the new baby's room and clothes. All the adults in that child's life are talking about the new baby coming. But what is the child thinking? Their thinking and ideas are realized in their play. The intention for that child is to understand that there is a baby coming. The child begins to play "having a baby" or engages in baby play.

This is not a passive interest. This is real research in which the child is trying to understand how that baby will come, what will happen in their life when that baby arrives, and how the family will take care of that baby. Over and over, the child will play having a baby, going to the doctor, and taking care of the baby. They will play this until their intentions are fully realized. They will play a hundred different ways of caring for a baby and having a baby.

Play in Action

A child was throwing objects and materials across the room and outside on the playground. He would throw his shoes, blocks, and even rocks. He was constantly doing this, and sometimes the objects hit other children and hurt them. He was never angry or mad when he was doing this. When we observed him closely, we saw he was joyful. So we paused and considered what he was doing. This was our moment as educators to dive into research with this child. What were his intentions? What was he trying to figure out? Finally, after about a week of this, we realized that he was trying to figure out how objects travel through the air. He was investigating the *trajectory* play schema—the movement of materials and bodies.

Once we realized what he was doing, we started talking about trajectory and catapults and how they work and how objects fly. We researched catapults with him and read stories about catapults. We started building catapults and targets together. He soon understood how materials traveled through the air and at a target, and he quickly realized how big, heavy rocks fly slowly and how little rocks travel very quickly. His work caught the attention of other children also, so the play became positive as he built catapults with other children and fulfilled his need to investigate how materials travel through the air.

For the child to be able to speak or show you their ideas through play schemas, they must feel safe to assert their meaning-making of the world. Many children grow up in environments where they don't feel this kind of emotional safety. For some, self-expression is met with criticism, or they are told that it's the wrong answer or it's silly or cute. Our job as educators is to say, "I would never have thought of that" or "Let's think about that for a minute" or "What do you think?"

We as educators should give children as many opportunities as possible to freely participate in the daily experiences of a school. We need to reject the prevailing practice of defining a child by their assessments or competencies or cuteness. These underestimate a child's real intentions in the world.

Likewise, worksheets do not speak to children's intentions, thinking, or ideas. Instead, it is our job to realize children's many ideas and intentions, notice them, hear them, and help them to co-construct with us. Our real work comes about by listening, observing, and recording their intentions. Noticing the intention is an important part of our job as educators to fully realize a project and discover what the children are trying to figure out.

How do we notice their intentions? Journals are an important part of my daily work with children. I record what they say. I record the play and materials that fascinate them. I also record my ideas about what comes next and what I think they are trying to figure out.

Using Verbs in Project Work

As I have studied and researched intentions of young children through my observations and hands-on work with them, I have come to understand that the verb in play schemas holds high value in project work or inquiry-based play. Keeping verbs at the heart of project work has become a central part of our Reggio-inspired practice at the Sunflower School.

Focusing on verbs in play-based learning and project work was part of a discussion at the Acorn School in Richmond Hill, Ontario, in 2015. During this professional development event, educators shared their thoughts about project work and how to make it more meaningful. We wanted to move away from themes and into project work, or *progettazione*, as it is called in Reggio-inspired practice. How could this happen and how could we do this research? We talked about nouns versus verbs as projects, and I was fascinated by the idea that project work is about constructing and building theories and ideas, so therefore a project is a verb, not a noun.

Nouns have been the traditional way of organizing themes such as *community helpers* or *recycling trucks* or *ladybugs*. Nouns are linear, whereas verbs have life and action. Projects too should have movement and be active and grow and expand as our ideas grow and expand. When projects are based on nouns, they are narrow and limiting and can be one-dimensional. Verbs are dynamic and three-dimensional. And projects should be three-dimensional, with many different perspectives.

Verbs give us a different viewpoint than the nouns we see in our world. The verb in the play tells us what children are engaged in, constructing, or thinking about. Instead of looking at a recycling truck that pulls up to your school every week and thinking that the children are interested in the recycling truck as a noun or a theme, look at it from a verb's point of view. How does it move? How does it make the enormous noise? How do the truck wheels move? What are the mechanics of the truck? And where does the garbage go?

It's not the recycling truck itself that we build the project on but rather the large, loud movement of the truck. Most recycling trucks have mechanisms that pick up the bins, and children

find this magical. The movement is the fascination, and therefore *moving* is the verb that becomes the foundation of the inquiry-based learning. This is a bigger and more complex project than the simple theme of *recycling truck*. What else moves in a big and enormous way? What moves in small ways? You can expand the project to explore different types of movement, such as flying, floating, rolling, swimming, running, jumping, or animal movements. This project could also be about listening to the sounds in our world, since the sound of the recycling truck is big, loud, and fascinating to most toddlers.

Many preschoolers are fascinated with rainbows. In my own teacher's research, I have found that happy children draw a lot of rainbows. Rainbows are magical and magnificent. But *rainbow* is a noun. We can draw, we can paint, and we can see the colors in the rainbows—but a project about rainbows is limited and does not involve critical or creative thinking. However, we can begin a project based on the verb of rainbows,

transforming, when we ask how the sky transforms into a rainbow. The verb of *transforming* holds the magic.

Transforming is a play schema. *Transforming* is about discovering how materials turn into something else: how flour and water turn into playdough or how light and rain turn into a rainbow. *Transforming* is about scientific critical thinking. This is where magical thinking happens, an intersection of scientific investigation and creative thinking. Children love to investigate rainbows through materials and science experiments. How do rainbows form? How can we transform these materials (light and a mirror, prism, or water) into a rainbow? The power you give children when they can offer their own ideas and create their own rainbows is magical.

This is the play in action in the life of a project. Your questions as a teacher-researcher build on that project. You can create many play proposals about creating a rainbow. Transforming rainbows is only part of this enormous project. How do seeds transform into flowers? How do caterpillars transform into butterflies? How does winter transform into spring? How does a green leaf transform into a colorful red leaf?

I use the bug story from *The Hundred Languages of Children* by Carolyn Edwards, Lella Gandini, and George Forman as another example of turning a noun into a verb into an in-depth project (2012, 164). The story features a group of children who find a bug in their block area. The children watch with joy as the bug moves and crawls in the block creations. The way the bug moves is fascinating for them.

As I read the story, I thought about the children I have worked with over the years and how bugs on our playground have caused the same joy and excitement. I wondered, "How can I take this story of the bug—a common theme in our environments both indoors and outdoors—and transform it into a long-term project?" What really fascinated the children about the bugs was the way they moved. How can something so small move so fast? Where are they going? So one of the first questions I would pose to the children would be "Are the bugs lost?" Then I would wait for the children's answers and ideas.

One big idea that comes to my mind is *mapping*, which is part of many kindergarten and preschool curricula. The noun, *bug*, was the vehicle to get to the richer and more important project work of the verb, *mapping*. Asking the right question at the right time could be a step into magical work for your children and yourself.

Let's now contrast the simpler work that happens with themes with the more complex work that can happen when we look deeper into the children's play and notice what they are fascinated with.

Traditional Theme-Based Activities

After the brief exchange about the bug, a teacher will decide to create a theme on bugs:

- Read stories about bugs.
- Paint or glue on precut bug shapes.
- Play with plastic bugs in waterplay or with playdough.
- Add bug manipulatives to math and science areas.

But if we think more deeply about what is actually fascinating to the children, our work can become more interesting and full of research that includes both the children and the educators.

Reggio-Inspired Research Projects

The teacher watches the children with the bug for a significant amount of time. The teacher takes photos and/or videos and records the children's ideas and conversations in a journal. Then the project unfolds:

- We can create a teacher research question that will guide the children and the project: "How can a bug find its way in the world?"
- To solve our question, first we can ask, "How do *we* find our way when we are lost?" Children can answer this question, and they can also interview parents, family members, or other teachers in the school about how they find their way when they are lost.
- Likely these interviews will introduce words like *GPS* or *maps*, leading us to ask how we might create a map for a bug.
- This leads to investigating real maps. For example, we may read books about mapping, examine maps of the community, and make a map of the school.

- Then we start to draw maps with the children. How do maps work? What signs are on the road? Why do we need signs? Why do we need roads? Perhaps we can watch roads being asphalted.
- We can take walks in our community and bring a map. We can also talk about street signs and house and building numbers.
- We can ask, "Where was the bug going? How does the bug find its home?" This allows us to create stories with the children about a bug getting lost and finding its way.
- We can also think about a bug city with the children. What do we have in our own city or community? Children can start to draw these bug cities, then create them into 3D models with various types of clay or natural materials.

There is obviously more than one way to think about this bug in a block center and many verbs to investigate. For example, the children could think about how we care for other living things in our world. Then this verb of *caring* becomes the focus of the project.

If we look at the very traditional community helper themes, for example, we can convert those words into verbs:

- *Caring*: displaying kindness and concern for others.
- *Helping*: giving assistance or support to someone or something; a helper is someone who puts others first in an altruistic way.

When I think of play schemas and community helpers, I think of *transforming*: turning unsafe or unpleasant situations into positive situations for people, like putting out a fire. How do we put out a fire? How do firefighters put out fires? How does a fire hydrant work?

The research questions and work are full of potential. How can our children help others in our community? How can we create drawings to thank our community helpers or people working in the hospitals? How can we help our friends get bundled up in the winter or put on shoes? How can we transform others' lives by collecting winter gear for people in need? This project work would be filled with many opportunities and possibilities for learning about how to help people. It allows us to build citizens of tomorrow who are kind and helpful, rather than just asking them to paint on a precut fire truck.

The staff and I have often brainstormed ways to convert nouns into verbs for project work. The planning sheet in appendix A will help you convert the nouns you observe in children's play into verbs. Educators bring in words that interest the children in their classrooms or that interest them in their research—something they are observing or noticing. Maybe educators have already started to think about projects as verbs, but we can become more intentional as we create webs of ideas. Webs are a way to dump all your ideas and thinking from the children onto paper. The web below gives you an example of how to create a web of ideas.

Verbs have a powerful perspective that will expand and extend your work with inquiry-based learning. Nouns have a place in inquiry-based learning as a vehicle to expand on the verb, such as in the stories about recycling trucks, ladybugs, or rainbows. Your work will have more meaning, and children will become more fully immersed when you use verbs.

Reflective Questions

In your work, how do you observe children's play?

After reading this chapter, where do you see the verbs in children's play? How could you start to notice the verbs in inquiry-based learning, as opposed to nouns?

How might your practice change as you notice the differences between the verb and the noun in inquiry-based learning?

Do you see play schemas in your children's play? If you identify a play schema in their play, create a web supporting the play schema to help children extend their play.

How could the play schemas in chapter 1 expand and extend your work with young children?

How can you use the template in appendix A, which outlines a process for converting nouns to verbs, in your work with children?

CHAPTER 2

Incorporating Play Schemas into Curriculum

LISA AGOGLIATI

> Children's schemas, which illuminate their patterns of behavior and thought, can open the door to a wealth of learning opportunities. When professionals are able to identify children's interests in this way, they are better placed to select appropriate curricular provision because their work is more clearly informed by knowledge of theory and of children's development.
>
> —Cathy Nutbrown

While early childhood curricula vary, as do the ways learning experiences are designed and implemented in schools, young children in these environments share a huge commonality: they *all* play. Play, especially during ages two to five, is the vehicle for how children naturally explore their world. Questions arise from children's engagement with objects that propel the play into patterns or categories of movement, such as *transporting, rolling, dropping,* or *filling*. The children discover answers, as educator Alexis Ralphs states, "one action at a time" (2023).

Supporting Explorations and Investigations with Play Schemas

Broadly speaking, early childhood curriculum is designed to support young children in learning about their world. With units or investigations around noun-based topics such as *weather, community helpers,* or *insects,* the inquiry might begin with gathering prior knowledge and then following the flow of questions, either as specifically outlined with published material or as devised by teachers based on their interpretations of the children's interests.

However, as seen in the previous chapter, we often increase the children's interest when we create learning experiences around verbs, rather than nouns, and when we connect the prominent actions of the children's play to the curriculum topic. Incorporating play schemas to guide the direction of a potential investigation promotes authentic opportunities for the children to discover a deeper connection between their own actions of play and the world.

For example, a pre-K team at NCRC collected observations about children's conversations about wind and was planning an investigation on weather. I asked them about the schema patterns they had seen in the children's play, which they said followed the actions of *rotation/circularity*. With this observation in mind, I asked them to consider how this schema could be used in their planning. They encouraged conversations at whole-group times to include stories of the children's recent repeated actions of turning on the playground, connecting to the movement of wind tunnels and turbines.

As Susan Stacey reminds us, "Small yet wonderful moments of learning unfold around us every day" (2023, 18). Sometimes one child's discovery has a ripple effect on other children's curiosity. NCRC preschool teachers Hitomi Inoue and Kelsey O'Brien experienced such a moment and recognized it as an opportunity to support further exploration using play schemas.

Play in Action

During the beginning of the school year, our dramatic play included a variety of clothing, including a sequined dress. An unexpected moment occurred when a child wearing the dress stood in front of a window on a sunny day and noticed the array of sparkly shapes moving around the room as he moved his body. The other students were fascinated by the light and took turns wearing the dress and walking around the classroom. After sharing this documentation with Lisa, we discussed how the schema of *orientation/perspective* could be used to support an exploration of light.

Inspired by this extraordinary moment, we wanted to create opportunities to look at what the children were doing beyond wearing the dress. As we added more shimmery fabric to dramatic play, the children sought to replicate the effect of sparkles projecting across the room. When they noticed that the reflections were harder to find on a cloudy and rainy day, their discovery extended our investigation with their personal hypotheses. So we set forth different invitations, such as placing mirrors and disco balls around the classroom and supplying flashlights for the children to create reflections on holographic paper, geodes, and mirrors. Through these invitations, the children learned about how different surfaces can be reflective or not. After learning about visual artist Yayoi Kusama, who uses reflections to create Infinity Mirror Rooms, children experimented with multiple mirrors to create infinite reflections, using battery-powered candles as light sources. Responding to this special encounter by using the *perspective* play schema to support our initial exploration of light became a rich, meaningful, and mesmerizing seven-week-long investigation.

—Hitomi Inoue and Kelsey O'Brien

Play in Action

Our Early Learning teaching team (ages two to three) had identified from our notes the children's interest in dinosaurs. After initially talking with the children about sizes of dinosaurs and what dinosaurs eat, we wondered where the exploration might lead. Lisa encouraged us to offer an invitation with loose parts and small dinosaur figures and to look for the specific actions of the children's play and conversations. Do the children use materials to create tall stacks for the dinosaurs to climb and jump off of? Or manipulate them into enclosures? Are they fascinated with stomping dinosaurs on the ground or flying them through the air? Opening and closing a dinosaur's mouth?

Our observations over the next week showed play (both with the children's bodies and with materials) that incorporated flying, running, and stomping throughout the room and playground. Our notes also included children's language; for example, one child referred to how a dinosaur with wings "flew up and then went down in

the sand," as they demonstrated that motion. At this point, our team decided to shift away from the noun of *dinosaurs* into the specific language of *trajectory* and paths of movement.

Our initial plan for a week of different invitations of *trajectory* included bubbles, balls, and stomp rockets. However, once we introduced the bubbles, the children demonstrated such fascination with how they traveled along a path in the air that we decided to slow down even further. We allowed time for the children to fully experience the action of blowing bubbles (the trajectory of their breath into the bubble wand) and then watching how the bubbles moved along a path. They compared the paths of little and big bubbles and watched what happened when they blew bubbles with fast, medium, or slow breaths. When we asked about how the bubbles were moving, we noticed the children used their hands to show pathways in the air of moving up, down, or side to side.

We then offered an art project where we took photos of each student practicing blowing bubbles and watching the path of their bubbles. The photo was glued along the edge of the paper so the children could use the space to illustrate their bubble path using marks made by dipping a plastic tube into paint and drawing the path with an oil pastel. The children's enthusiastic response to this initial exploration of pathways gave way to a rich investigation over the next several weeks, extending into learning about animals that follow paths on land, in the water, and in the air.

—**Katie Deane Brophy and Laura Sheedy**

Whether children are playing with a specific idea, such as dinosaurs, or playing with representational toys, such as dinosaur figures, they have intentions within their play that are based in schemas. Although children are intrinsically motivated to explore these different actions, educators may have to refamiliarize themselves with these same tools (schemas) we once used ourselves as young children. As we reconnect to these ways of thinking, the children's intentions become clearer to us and play more of a role in our reflection on the curriculum. Educators' observations of schemas in the children's play can then be used to interpret their intentions and support new invitations or explorations of ideas both inside and outside the classroom.

Since children regularly explore multiple schemas, having a couple of areas in the classroom with neutral materials allows them to express ideas outside of the main curriculum topic. Or in some cases, it allows them to apply knowledge gained during the investigation or unit of study. Blocks, open-ended purchased manipulatives (such as Magna-Tiles or Lego bricks), and clay are common examples of materials that allow for different kinds of schema play.

Incorporating loose parts with these materials can also spark schema play. Loose parts are everyday items that are manipulated by children in an open-ended way. Objects made of paper, plastic, metal, nature items, or fabric offer rich sensory experiences and allow children's intentions to unfold in a myriad of actions, such as rolling, stacking, balancing, lining up, looking through, and enclosing.

Connecting/Disconnecting

Enclosing

Rotation

Trajectory

Positioning

Perspective

Transforming

Transporting

When arranging tables or centers to feature open-ended materials, I encourage teachers to observe the following:

- Do the children use neutral materials when engaging in play related to the current investigation or study?
- Do the children use neutral materials to express new play ideas not related to the current investigation or study topic?

In environments that follow emergent curriculum, teachers' observations of play schemas, as seen through children's play with open-ended materials, can be used to deepen investigations. Educators may use their observations to introduce a new aspect as well as to help interpret whether the children's interest remains with the current investigation or is perhaps leading to something new. I encourage teachers to observe to answer these questions:

- What patterns of movement are the children creating with the materials?
- How might those specific play schemas be used to deepen the current investigation or project in a new way?

For example, when a team was several weeks into an investigation of the rainforest, they began to wonder whether they should stay longer on the topic and, if so, what that might look like. They had observed that the children were asking fewer questions while looking at rainforest books. They had also noticed that the children were less frequently choosing to play in the dramatic play area, which featured toy rainforest animals and a visual rainforest the children had constructed.

When I asked them about their other non-rainforest invitations, they shared that the children continued to spend time with dolls, especially carrying and taking care of babies. In this situation, having observed the prominent schema of *transporting* through the children's engagement with the dolls, the educators could apply the schema to introduce a new aspect to the rainforest topic, asking how rainforest animals travel with and care for their young. Instead of wrapping up the investigation, the team planned for the following week to make explicit connections from their observations of the children's actions with the dolls to wondering about and examining the ways animals in the rainforest carry their babies. The result not only introduced relevant information on the current topic but also showed the value of taking time with transitions.

You can follow a similar practice by using the framework in appendix B to brainstorm ways to extend play investigations with schemas.

Juicy Verbs

To ensure play schemas' success in the environment, educators should intentionally introduce and use schema vocabulary when naming the action(s) they see, regardless of whether they use published material or follow an emergent approach. A key part of my work is to use what I like to call "juicy verbs" when talking with a child or small group about the actions (schemas) I observe in their play.* I point out and intentionally name the action using descriptive verbs related to the schema or add to the language they are using. I then refer to these new words later with the whole group as an invitation to explore a specific action further and expand our schema-related vocabulary.

I encourage teachers to print out large photos of the children's play that illustrate the schema idea in action and then ask the child(ren) to describe what is happening in the photos. Teachers can use these moments to layer in additional schema vocabulary for the particular action.

Other times, the juicy verbs will spring up right in the moment of play. For example, a child spent a long time during outside play finding a particular leaf that would work for his idea to "wrap up" several magnolia seeds. Other children noticed

*I originally learned about the term *juicy words* from my work in theater education with Dr. Gail Humphries and David Markey. They used *juicy* when endowing a word with a sense of taste or touch to make it clear and understood. I adapted this term to use when referencing a set of descriptive verbs related to the formal schema name (i.e., *enclosing*) in ways that made the meaning clear for young children.

the little package when he showed a teacher, and soon they began their own *wrapping* quests on the playground.

Later at a whole-group gathering, I invited him to demonstrate the sequence of steps he followed. This sharing also allowed me to add more vocabulary to the conversation, such as *folding* and *enclosing*.

Later we honored his word choice of *wrap* with an invitation asking, "What can you wrap with a leaf?" at a classroom center. The center

encouraged a See, Think, Wonder thinking routine, which asks, "What do you see? What do you think about that? What does it make you wonder?" (Project Zero 2022).

Sometimes a particular schema is highly visible throughout the action in the classroom. For example, a teaching team observed that the focus of the children's play was moving many kinds of toys from one area to the next. We discussed what it would look like to take photos of this pattern and then use them to begin a conversation with the group, incorporating juicy verbs: "We noticed you have been *carrying* the toys (or materials) to different places in the classroom. You have been *transporting* them with your hands back and forth. What else could you use to *move* them to different parts of the classroom?" Following the discussion, we offered invitations to explore materials of different sizes. We also offered toy manipulatives with parts that have wheels and established start/end areas to get the children thinking about how the materials could move from one place to another.

As older students demonstrate their understanding of schemas and begin to incorporate schema vocabulary, suddenly it can seem as though the action is everywhere! In one case, a pre-K class's ongoing discovery of *enclosing* yielded so many juicy verbs from the children that teachers created an ongoing list:

cover	enfold	cage
encase	wrap	hug
enclose	veil	fence
surround	conceal	cuddle
blanket	swaddle	trap

The following are some of my favorite juicy verbs to use with various schemas.

Schema Category	Juicy Verbs
Transporting	Carry, cart, tow, push, pull, move, deliver, ship, bring, lift, funnel, transplant, pack, lug, tote, transfer, haul, take, slide, drag, roll, flip
Transforming	Change, convert, shift, mold, reconstruct, remodel, transfer, make, create, imagine, pretend, replace, swap, trade, build, sculpt, construct, move, replace, morph, evolve
Connecting	Put together, combine, join, hitch, fuse, hook, interlock, attach, strap, snap, tie, tape, glue, button, toggle, join, link, weave
Disconnecting	Detach, untie, untangle, take apart, separate, release, break up, disassemble, remove, break down, unfasten
Rotating/Circling	Turn, spin, roll, twirl, pivot, wheel, swivel, whirl, orbit, repeat, move around, wind, twist, curl, revolve, swing, crank, spiral, loop
Enclosing/Enveloping	Wrap, wind, seal up, box up, box in, wall in, fence, frame, surround, contain, include, fit, cocoon, cover, spread out, swaddle, hide inside, disguise, close, tuck, fill, flood, heap
Orientation/Perspective	See, look at, notice, view, angle, look through, observe, examine, explain, change, look like, understand, stand
Positioning/Ordering	Arrange, choose, line up, place, set, balance, assemble, lay out, layer, organize, sort, group, line up, map out, decide
Trajectory	Fly, spring, project, arc, track, loop, circle, extend, reach, aim, curve, launch, motion, move, accelerate, increase, leap, vault, plunge, drop, throw, jump, pounce
Aggregating	Gather, collect, assemble, heap, pile, layer, cluster, group, herd, bunch up, bring together, bundle, flock
Moving through Boundaries	Poke, make holes, dig, strain, button, pass through, tunnel, burrow, excavate, scoop out, hollow out, dredge, uncover, root out, harvest, drill

Using Schemas with Published Curriculum

Using play schemas is not limited to emergent curriculum that uses investigations or project-based work. With flexible curriculum frameworks such as The Creative Curriculum, teachers can select a variety of designed studies that meet the current interests of their students. Each teaching guide helps educators meet curriculum standards and create a responsive environment.

In reviewing Creative Curriculum's studies, I noticed that many were based on nouns, such as pets, bread, sand, insects, boxes, and roads. I challenged myself to look at a progression of curriculum units and think of ideas for how schemas could be used as a transition tool between each unit, also considering what I might include in the Discovery Center, which is part of the Creative Curriculum classroom environment.

Two approaches to using schemas for this purpose came to mind:

1. Teachers could identify a schema from a concept in a previous study that could connect with an element in the next study.
2. Teachers could identify a schema from the children's play that could connect with an element in the next study.

For example, say a teacher was planning a transition for a class (ages three to four years) from the Light Study to the Exercise Study. Among the last activities in the Light Study were exploring the effects of light and shadow and discovering what kinds of things light can shine through. We can see the schema of *perspective/orientation* in this area of the curriculum. Common to the beginning of a Creative Curriculum study is gathering information from the children on what they know about the topic. An interesting transition to this discussion could be to structure the conversation linking the two with language from the schema of *perspective/orientation*.

<table>
<tr><th>Schema Category</th><th colspan="2">Juicy Verbs</th></tr>
<tr><td>Orientation/Perspective</td><td colspan="2">See, look, notice, view, angle, look through, observe, examine, explain, change, look like, understand, stand, think, position</td></tr>
<tr><td>Orientation/ Perspective Connections from Light Study
• What did you notice about the position of the sun when we observed our shadows outside?
• How did the shape of the light look when you held the flashlight down low or up high?
• What happened to the shape of the object when you moved the light source closer or far away?</td><td>Orientation/ Perspective Connections to Exercise Study
• What kinds of exercise can people do when their bodies are positioned on the ground?
• What kinds of exercise can people do when they reach up high with their bodies?
• What kind of exercise equipment do people use that stays in place? That moves them from one place to another?</td><td>Orientation/ Perspective Connections to Children's Play & Life Experiences
• When you are playing on the playground equipment, how does your perspective change when you stand on the top of a climber? Hang upside down on the monkey bars?
• What kinds of healthy snacks do you like to eat?
• How would you move your body from one place to another from the perspective of being a baby, child, adult, or old person?</td></tr>
</table>

Similarly, educators using Creative Curriculum could also use their observations of the schemas in children's play that relate to the next study that includes that repeated action. For example, in preparing for a transition to the Insects Study after spring break, a teacher had noticed many of her children rolling, spinning, and moving round and round the slide during outdoor play. We talked about how she could connect the *rotating* schema observed in her children's play to the start of the Insect Study by exploring local insects such as pill bugs that roll up and millipedes that spiral.

In addition, we discussed how she could connect the concept of *rotation* to their earlier Exercise Study by asking the children to recall which types of exercise use equipment that spins or rolls, such as bikes, Rollerblades, or roller skates. We also brainstormed schema connections that stemmed from her observations inside the classroom. She noticed that in the dramatic play center—which included a kitchen, play food, dress-ups, and baby dolls—children were engaging in play scenarios of family, restaurant, beauty salon, and riding a train. Our follow-up conversation included specific ideas for the teacher to identify the prominent *actions* the children were doing when playing out these scenarios:

- Is the focus of the family play about *ordering/positioning*? That is, is there an emphasis on who is the dad, mom, baby, or older or younger sibling? Or is the focus on *enclosing* by swaddling a baby or sleeping in a bed?
- Is the focus of the restaurant play about *transporting* food items from the kitchen to a customer? Or is the emphasis on *enclosing* by placing food inside an oven or covering a pot on the stove?
- Is the focus of the beauty salon on *transforming* with haircuts? Or are children fascinated with the *rotation* of tools for curling hair?
- Is the focus of the rides on trains the *trajectory* of the path/speed they are traveling on? Or are they more interested in *transporting* things from one place to another?

Once identified, play schemas can be applied to the current investigation, such as the Insects Study. Here are some examples:

- If the family play is about *ordering/positioning*, you could look at insect classification or the roles bees and ants have in their communities.
- If the restaurant play includes a focus on *transporting*, you could look more into how insects carry food.
- If the beauty salon play reveals a lot of *rotation*, you could learn about the dung beetle, which rolls large balls of dung.
- If the train play reflects *trajectory*, you could examine the fast movement of dragonflies or tiger beetles.

Emily Paterson, an experienced practitioner from the District of Columbia Public Schools, shares her reflections on pairing Creative Curriculum with schemas.

Play in Action

Creative Curriculum provides essential questions, investigations, text suggestions, and ideas for center activities and materials for each of its studies, but it also preserves space for teacher autonomy and allows flexibility to follow student interests. With Lisa's encouragement, I referenced actions from the previous Exercise Study to make another connection to the new Insects Study. For example, during the Exercise Study they were practicing doing forward rolls with their bodies. When we transitioned to insects, I showed them how pill bugs roll up into a ball and said, "It's just like you when you were practicing your somersaults!" At recess the children continued to explore orientation by hanging upside down on the monkey bars. I referenced this action when we began the Insects Study by pointing out how a butterfly chrysalis hangs from a stick the same way they hang from the monkey bars. To help the children connect this specific action to the study, we ordered some caterpillars and observed as they climbed up the walls and built chrysalides that hung from the top. They also enjoyed acting out a song about caterpillar metamorphosis.

During the study I noticed a lot more engagement with the topics of investigation when I connected them with play schemas. However, young children's learning never stays narrowly focused, and as always, there were children whose play centered on their preferred interests, such as vehicles and doll babies. Lisa encouraged me to look deeply at the actions of their play scenarios and determine the focus of their play so I could connect it to our study investigations. In the dramatic play center, the children had recently been playing beauty salon with the baby dolls. The actions of their play suggested they were interested in *transformation*, so I related it to insect metamorphosis, and we discussed how a larva becoming a beetle was like getting a big makeover. I incorporated a lot of juicy verbs to build their vocabulary of *transformation* and was excited when they could use the same verbs later in the study to describe how insects transform dead plants and animals through decomposition!

Learning about play schemas gave me a new lens with which to understand the play scenarios I see most often in our classroom. It was easy to create invitations to play in our existing centers based on the actions we noticed and then tie those into the essential questions of our studies. I see play schema work as a tool to deepen students' engagement with the Creative Curriculum investigations. It helped build their vocabulary and strengthen connections, and it allowed me to introduce more neutral materials to centers rather than rely on strictly theme-based activities. I am looking forward to incorporating this new perspective in my future work.

—Emily Paterson

See appendix C for more ideas on using play schemas as transition tools within a flexible curriculum framework such as the Creative Curriculum.

In structured thematic-based curriculum, such as the Frog Street curriculum, the units have a set order for educators to follow. The use of schemas in this setting can highlight the children's actions in play in a new way as it relates to the next unit. For instance, educators can plan the transition from Color, Shape, and Size to the study of Safe and Healthy Me by identifying the common schema of *enclosing/enveloping* to bridge one study to the next.

Color: What happened when you *covered* the yellow piece of cellophane with the blue piece at the light table?

Shapes: What shapes did we discover *fit inside* the diamond?

Size: How many different sizes of Matryoshka dolls were *tucked* in the largest doll?

As the group transitions to the new unit, schema connections to *enclosing/enveloping* can be used as a starting point to gather prior knowledge:

Safe Me: What is something you use to *cover* your head when riding your bike?

Healthy Me: Where are bones, muscles, and the heart *enclosed* in your body?

Eating Well: What fruits or vegetables are *enclosed* in something we need to remove before eating?

Educators can also use prominent schemas observed directly from children's play as a bridge between planned studies. For example, if there was a noticeable pattern of *lining up/positioning* in the children's play, teachers could incorporate this action into a review of the previous Color, Shape, and Size unit:

Color: How can we *line up* these color swatches from dark to light?

Shape: What patterns can we *design* with these different shapes?

Size: Can you *balance* a big object on a small object?

As the group transitions to the new unit, schema connections to *positioning/ordering* can be used as a starting point to gather prior knowledge:

Safe Me: How do we *line up* when we have a fire drill at school? What is the order of the colors on a stoplight?

Healthy Me: How do we *sequence* our routine for washing hands?

Eating Well: How can we *arrange* these foods to follow the MyPlate healthy eating guidelines?

Active Me: How can we *organize* ways our body can move in a pattern?

Here is an example of a chart that illustrates using schemas to transition between Frog Street units:

<table>
<tr><th>Schema Category</th><th colspan="2">Juicy Verbs</th></tr>
<tr><td>Transporting</td><td colspan="2">Carry, cart, tow, push, pull, move, deliver, ship, bring, lift, funnel, transplant, pack, lug, tote, transfer, haul, take, slide, drag, roll, flip</td></tr>
<tr><td>Transporting Connections to On the Go unit
• Reread Boats Float!
• Which boats hauled large items?
• Which boats could transfer people?
• How does a tugboat help other vessels?</td><td>Transporting connections to Amazing Critters unit
• How does an ant carry food back to its home?
• How do bees deliver pollen back to the honeycomb?
• How do spiders tote their eggs sacs?</td><td>Transporting connections to Children's Play and Life Experiences
• How can you carry a rock with a stick or transport sand with a leaf?
• How many ways can you transport food from the grocery store to your home?
• What are the different ways a baby can be carried?</td></tr>
</table>

See appendix D for more ideas on play schemas as transition tools within structured thematic-based curriculum such as Frog Street.

Schema Connections with Literature

As educators identify prominent schemas in their specific project work, investigations, and unit activities, children's literature can be a rich tool for supporting, expanding, and connecting to schema vocabulary and for promoting children's recognition of juicy verbs.

For example, a team working with two- and three-year-olds was exploring the schema of *enclosing* as they followed the children's fascination with the idea that someone or something can disappear by being hidden. During this time, the teachers were also introducing the author Ezra Jack Keats. The children had noticed in *The Snowy Day* and *A Letter to Amy* that Willie the dog was often hidden behind something. I asked the team what it would be like to reread these stories with a focus on *enclosing* as it relates to Willie. The team's directing teachers, Sarah Chatzkel and Carolee Clay, told me how the children responded to this new focus:

Teacher: *Where is Willie?*

Child A: *He is inside the box!*

Child B: *I see his head.*

Child C: *He is behind it.*

Teacher: *Where is the rest of his body?*

Child D: *It is gone.*

Child A: *It is behind the box.*

Teacher: *Where is Willie on this page?*

Child A: *Willie is tucked in the wall . . . ?*

Teacher: *What part of Willie is missing?*

Child A: *The bow!* [referring to the collar]

Teacher: *What part do you see?*

Child A: *The legs!*

Teacher: *And where is Willie on this page?*

Child B points to Willie.

Teacher: *Is there anything near him?*

Child B: *His tail!*

Teacher: *Is he hiding?*

Child B: *Yes!*

Teacher: *How is he hiding?*

Child B: *Under the trash can!*

Teacher: *Is there a part of Willie missing?*

Child B: *His tail!*

The beautiful language of *tucked in*, along with the specific relationship of Willie's position (under, behind, and inside) generated by the children opened a whole new set of vocabulary. The team also noted the following:

> Upon introducing a stuffed animal of Willie, the children were fascinated by his collar. We talked a lot about how the collar was "wrapped" around him. The children then wanted to grab *A Letter to Amy* and find Willie (and his collar) in the book to make sure it matched. They really loved using the word *wrapped* during our group discussion. To demonstrate the word again, we wrapped Willie in a blanket. The children talked about how his "body was wrapped inside" and how the quilt was "on top of him."

Following the reading, a teacher noticed a few children playing inside a small structure on the playground. They were taking turns being in the middle and popping out. The teacher recognized this moment of schema in action and went over to intentionally connect their actions to the new word by pointing out that they were *tucked in*, where teachers couldn't see them—and then they popped out!

In settings where specific literature selections are included with the curriculum materials, educators can similarly apply the specific schema they have identified within the study. For example, *enclosing* is a prominent schema within the Creative Curriculum Clothes Study. The study begins with a look at the features of clothes, which supports a variety of *enclosing* vocabulary. The teacher could ask, "What kinds of clothes or fabric are worn by *wrapping* around the body?"

- bath towel
- blanket
- scarf
- baby swaddle
- Indian sari
- African headwrap

- hijab
- wedding veil

The discussion can then be expanded to look at how objects can be wrapped or enclosed in something. For example, the teacher can apply the lens of *enclosing/enveloping* to a rereading of the suggested read-aloud book *Abuela's Weave* by Omar S. Castaneda in the study's Investigation Part 3: "How do people make clothes?" Children can expand their understanding of the relationship between the schema and the topic as they reflect on different examples of *enclosing* they find in the story. As "*enclosing* detectives," they may discover the following examples from the opening page:

- a stone wall *surrounding* the house
- a basket *containing* yarn
- a scarf *wrapped* around Esperanza's head
- fields *filled* with corn, beans, and coffee
- jugs *holding* water
- sticks *wrapped* with yarn
- a thatched roof *covering* the house

Other published curricula with planned rereading of selected literature can utilize this same approach. For example, Frog Street's On the Go unit for Week 4's theme of Water includes rereading *The Zebra on the Zyder Zee.* One of the read-aloud sessions could invite the children to be "*transporting* detectives" as they identify different ways characters are carrying objects.

- How do you think the Zebra *moved* the barrels onto the boat? How would he move if he *pushed* or *pulled* them up the ramp?
- How does Bear *bring* his chest onto the boat? How would you *lift* a heavy case like Bear?
- What do Mama cat and her three babies *bring* onto the boat? How would you *carry* something if it had a handle or a strap?
- What makes the boat *move across* the ocean?

See appendix G for a resource list of play schemas and related children's literature.

Schema Connections with Social-Emotional Learning in Young Children

When I originally presented the idea of working with schemas to develop emergent curriculum to the NCRC faculty, one member approached me afterward to share a thought regarding possible relationships between schema categories and various components of social-emotional learning. Tarah Leroy, whose background includes a dual master's degree in early childhood and special education as well as more than ten years of teaching, offered a few ideas that instantly had me thinking of social-emotional development as another intersection with schema:

Play in Action

After working with preschool-aged children for many years, I have developed an interest in their social-emotional learning and how it translates to our work in the classroom. During Lisa's presentation regarding working with schemas to develop our curriculum, I could not help but think about how we can use these schemas to address the social-emotional needs of our students.

In the classroom, we work intentionally to create provocations that further develop their interests and their knowledge. It made sense to me that we could use these schemas as tools to intentionally meet our children where they were in their social-emotional development. There is power in schemas and in using a critical lens to discern what our children need to grow and learn. And as they grow in the classroom and develop friendships and relationships, we can observe that their social-emotional needs also deserve the same focus.

When we think of schemas, we tend to think of the act of play and the physical work associated with each schema. However, I also think it's important to dig a little deeper into their play and to pay attention to the social-emotional learning that occurs as each child explores a schema to make sense of their learning. Each exploration pushes each child to explore a part of their internal world and challenges them to collaborate, to self-regulate in moments of frustration, to recognize that they are part of a classroom community, and to make their own choices about how they play and what they do within their play. When we are being intentional with our provocations, we are also eliciting a social-emotional experience that may challenge our students to practice and develop the social skills necessary to engage in meaningful play.

For example, when we bring them artifacts of their time in the classroom, we are showing them how they have *transformed*—their interests, their friendships, themselves. When we engage our students in art projects that reflect classroom culture, we can address the schema of the *cumulative* or *aggregating*. For example, in studying textiles, each child can make an individual quilt square and the squares can be put together to create a classroom quilt that reflects the classroom community as a whole.

—Tarah Leroy

Tarah and I thought about how schema categories correspond to social-emotional learning components using the framework from the Collaborative for Academic, Social, and Emotional Learning (CASEL): self-awareness, self-management, social awareness, and relationship skills.

Self-awareness: The ability to accurately recognize one's emotions and thoughts and their influence on behavior.

This competency aligns with the *aggregating* schema. As a young child's self-awareness develops and expands from ages two to five, they build knowledge of themselves as a community member with their own tastes and ideas, and they grow beyond identifying favorite colors or foods to thinking about favorite places or people. As children expand their understanding of the range and depth of emotions, their emotional vocabulary range increases significantly, moving from a child expressing that they're feeling "mad" to specifically feeling "frustrated" or "disappointed."

Self-management: The ability to regulate one's emotions, thoughts, and behaviors effectively in different situations.

This competency reflects the *transforming* schema as young children are introduced to strategies they can use to manage their emotional and behavioral responses in different situations. The concept of change can be applied as young children gain experiences with applying mindful breathing, recalling language for their body's level of alertness as well as the level needed for specific tasks, recognizing visuals that support identifying their emotions, and following expectations within a group.

Social awareness: The ability to take the perspective of and empathize with others.

This competency supports the schema of *perspective/orientation*. This schema connects with play activities that incorporate open-ended materials as well as literature resources for introducing seeing, understanding, and appreciating differences.

Relationship skills: The ability to establish and maintain healthy and rewarding relationships with diverse individuals and groups.

This competency complements the schemas of *enclosing* and *connecting*. As young children learn the expectations of being part of a group, they come to recognize what can be achieved through the collective effort of each member. (See appendix F for resources with play schema connections to social-emotional learning concepts in the Social Thinking Methodology, the "How Does Your Engine Run?" Alert Program, and the Zones of Regulation curriculum.)

Teacher Hannah Schaefer recognized the value of using the schema of *enclosing* in connection with students' social-emotional skills with discussion prompts such as "How does enclosing promote belonging?"

Play in Action

The students in my pre-K class were struggling with social-emotional development around flexibility with friend groups and inclusion. There were some girls who had formed a tight friend group but excluded several other girls from joining in their play, and some boys who would decline to allow anyone to join in their outdoor dramatic play games involving superheroes. We also observed a lot of "You can't play with me" language. At the same time, the whole class was fascinated by the idea of *enclosing* and had been reflecting on how being enclosed in their homes or in their warm coats makes them feel. We talked about belonging and the feeling of being enveloped in the love of our families. Almost all of the students in this class were going on to new schools the following year, so reinforcing the idea of belonging and the reality of home being "where the love is" helped create a stronger sense of self and stability for the students and helped give them the strength to be resilient through the big changes coming their way.

The class asked lots of wondering questions about how homes enclose and reflected on how it makes them feel loved to have a home and community where they always belong. We spent time comparing and contrasting different homes around the world, from yurts in Mongolia to Housing Development Board (HDB) flats in Singapore to single-family homes in Washington, DC. In the spirit of homes that promote belonging, the class obtained and transformed a large cardboard box into a class cozy space. After painting it with paint sticks, they pasted decorated paper to the exterior, making it "fancy." Then, they added loose parts, ribbons, and cardboard cutouts. Lastly, they put pillows inside and used the space as a tiny home within our classroom, a place to relax and feel safe. Each day we noticed something had been added, taped, or glued on, as the students were constantly refining their creation. They were working together in groups, including the groups of girls and boys who had previously excluded their peers.

> Our thematic discussions and explorations of how being enclosed makes one feel and where enclosing occurs resulted in students being more accepting of one another, using more "You belong here" language.
>
> —Hannah Schaefer

Reflective Questions

How does the children's interaction with loose parts—the way they move the materials *and* themselves—change in the block area, the art area, or outside? What different schemas might the materials inspire?

How might your observations of a prominent schema be used to explore a potential idea for a project or investigation?

What are some methods you could use to help yourself slow down and watch for play schemas in young children?

How can you support children's relationship with and comprehension of schema actions through your incorporation of juicy verbs?

What would it look like to invite children to become "schema detectives" through a rereading of selected children's literature?

How could you apply a specific schema to your teaching of SEL concepts and related children's literature?

CHAPTER 3

Using Research Questions

HEATHER JACKSON

Ideas fly, bounce around, accumulate, rise up, fall apart, and spread until one of them takes a decisive hold and flies higher and conquers the entire group.

—Loris Malaguzzi

This quote shaped my thinking about questions and the countless ideas that come from both the children's ponderings and the teacher's research inquiries. The first part of the quote, "Ideas fly, bounce around, accumulate, rise up, fall apart, and spread," corroborates our understanding that verbs are the foundation of project work. The verbs in the quote are alive and full of action to help us act out the children's intentions and ideas in our classrooms.

Our project work at the Sunflower School always centers on the research question once the educators have gathered children's intentions from observations. Research is at the heart of our Reggio-inspired work. *Research* means to systemically investigate a line of ideas according to a plan. *Researching* is a verb, which supports the principle that verbs are the lines of investigation in project work or inquiry-based learning. The most important ingredient in research is the questions we create about the educators' and the children's intentions.

How does reflection change
when you add these
materials?
How will you make Light
Dance with these
materials?

The sprout's tail

How do you
follow a pattern?

The Language
of
Metal
How are you
inspired by
this material?

How Do Educators Ask Questions?

In our investigative work with children, we try to figure out the children's intentions: What are we adults noticing? What are the children wondering about? What are they playing repeatedly? And what have we noticed through a lens of play schemas or verbs?

The next step is asking how we turn the intentions of the action into rich, thought-provoking questions. We create questions for both the educators and the children because our research as educators is just as essential as the children's research. These research questions will guide your work with the children through the lines of investigation.

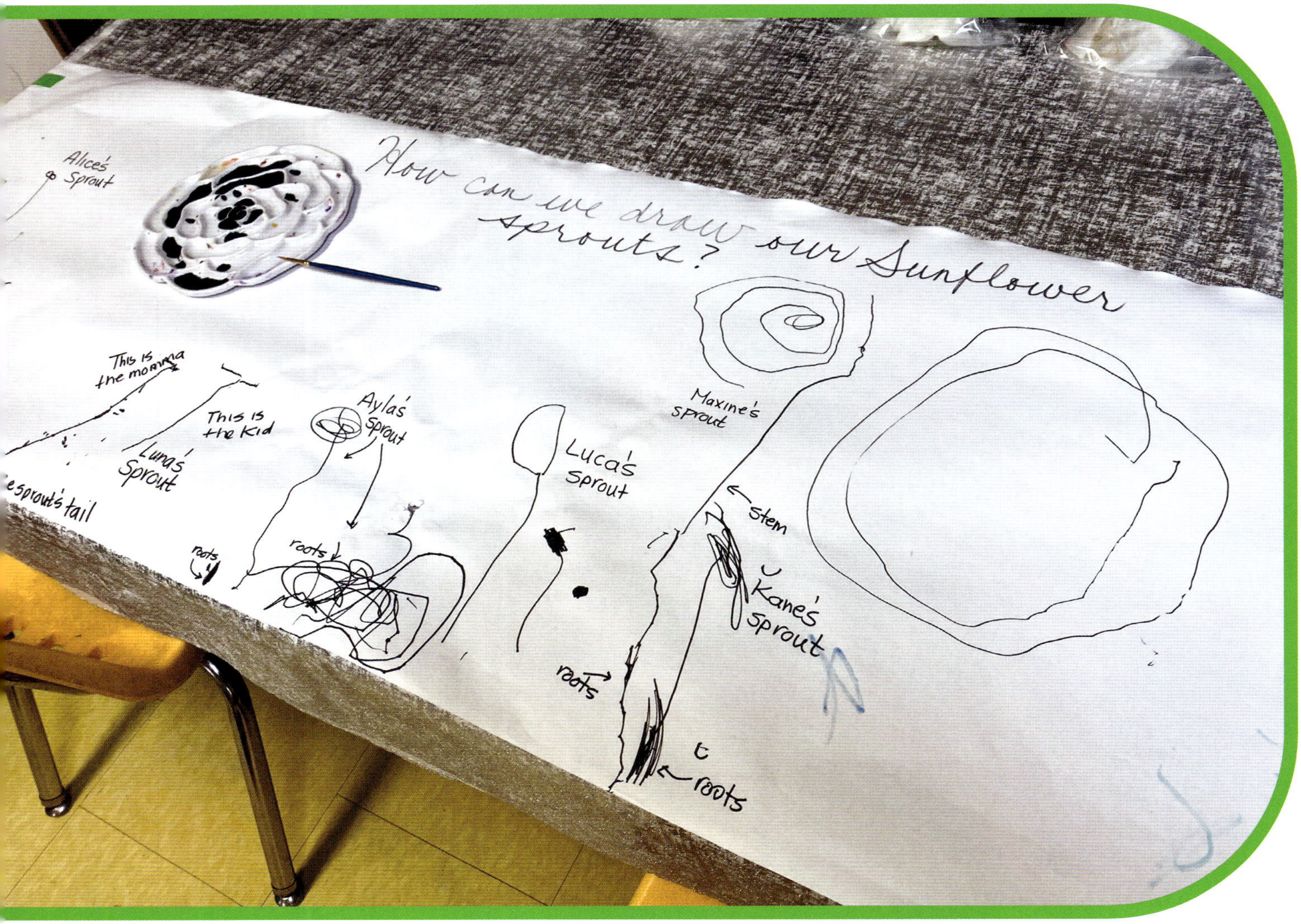

How might different
materials & supplies
inspire new &
magnificent ideas?

THE MOST
MAGNIFICENT
IDEA
How might we
combine & entangle
loose parts to create

Questions are made up of the 5*W*s. ***What*** questions are simply answered with facts, like "What can you build with these blocks?" The answer from a child could be "a tower," which does not lead to more interesting work. The questions we use for research must be detailed and elaborate so that we prompt enchanting ideas. We want children to untangle the question with magical thinking, but *what* questions can be simplistic. ***When*** questions are about a very specific time. ***Where*** questions are about a very specific place.

Why questions are about scientific concepts, and they require in-depth thought and fact finding. *Why* questions are developmentally appropriate for older children and key in exploring the world. We will more deeply consider *why* questions later in the chapter.

But ***how*** questions are about constructing ideas, building and engaging ideas, and, most important, about thinking magically, which is the basis for creative and critical thinking. Children do not have filters around their ideas, so their problem solving can be so creative. Children believe in the impossible. When a young child jumps off a rock or stump, I see the excitement in their faces, and I believe they think they will fly. We as educators need to hold that in our hearts and ask children the *how* questions for them to play in, so they can fly.

Creating *how* questions requires practice. The following are some starters for formulating *how* questions:

- How might we . . .
- How might I . . .
- How can we . . .
- How can you describe . . .
- How might you do it differently?
- How did you work together?
- How did you work it out?
- How can you brainstorm new ways to do it?
- How can we see this from another perspective?
- How did you build this?

How questions can have numerous answers—and this is exactly what you want as an educator. This may be uncomfortable for many people in early childhood, but I believe there is no right or wrong answer to these *how* questions (whatever science might say on the matter). We as educators sometimes want to know all the answers for our children, but I think about the magic that is created when children can express themselves in a hundred ways, figure out the world in a hundred ways, and live out their intentions in a hundred ways.

Every child's distinct perspective should be respected and heard by educators, so the children will ask any and all questions they have. When children say magical things in small-group times or during one-on-one moments, I tell them, "I never would have thought of that." This gives children power and confidence because they know that they have said something that their teacher, who typically holds the power, would never have thought of.

In the early days of the Sunflower School, an educator asked a group of preschoolers, "How do the leaves change color in the fall?" On our playground, we had the most beautiful sugar maple tree, and in the fall the color was a brilliant red. It was almost animated. Some of the answers were: "The weather changes the leaves," "The cold air," and "My mommy" (the all-powerful mommy). And then a very creative child said that the ladybugs land on the leaves and give the leaves their red color.

This child's explanation about the ladybug was so important in these educators' journeys. They were able to see how a child's simple but complex answer could launch a project. Using "How do leaves change color in the fall?" as the main research question, the children created their own stories of leaves changing colors; reenacted stories about ladybugs and leaves with loose parts; painted with beautiful shades of red that they mixed themselves; drew fall leaves with India ink, black Sharpie markers, and red watercolors; and played imaginatively with leaves and wooden ladybugs in our outdoor play area.

The educators did not need to answer the guiding research question with the scientific reasons why leaves change colors in the fall. The children did not memorize facts about the abundance of chlorophyll in leaves but rather imagined their own ideas about how they change color. Children will learn the scientific reasons in science classes as they get older. But for now, as preschoolers, they need to imagine their own ideas. For me, this recalls a quote from Albert Einstein: "Imagination is more important than knowledge. For knowledge is limited, whereas imagination embraces the world, stimulating progress, giving birth to evolution" (1931).

How Do Children Ask Questions?

When we start a new school year with older preschool and kindergarten children, we ask them, "How can we ask a beautiful question?" We begin by investigating and understanding the concept of questions so the children learn how to ask beautiful questions. During meeting times, we want children to be brave and ask interesting and important questions. If you, as the educator, ask a question that you already know the answer to, it is not a beautiful question.

Over the years, I have asked preschoolers questions during morning meeting times and have encouraged them to ask their own questions about the things they wonder about. When a child does ask a question, I will turn the conversation back to the other children and say, "What do we think about what Eliza just said?"

Asking questions is an important form of communication. For humans, communication is part of our belonging, well-being, expression, and engagement with the world. *Belonging* is a sense of fitting in or feeling like you are a part of a group. When we engage with other people through talking, pointing, gesturing, or singing, we feel a sense of belonging with that other person.

When children learn to ask questions, they start to feel a sense of connection with their educators and other children. *Well-being* is a sense of being comfortable, healthy, and happy. Children will ask and answer questions when they feel comfortable. Educators support and help them feel that state of comfort when children ask and answer questions. We are giving validation to children's ideas and questions.

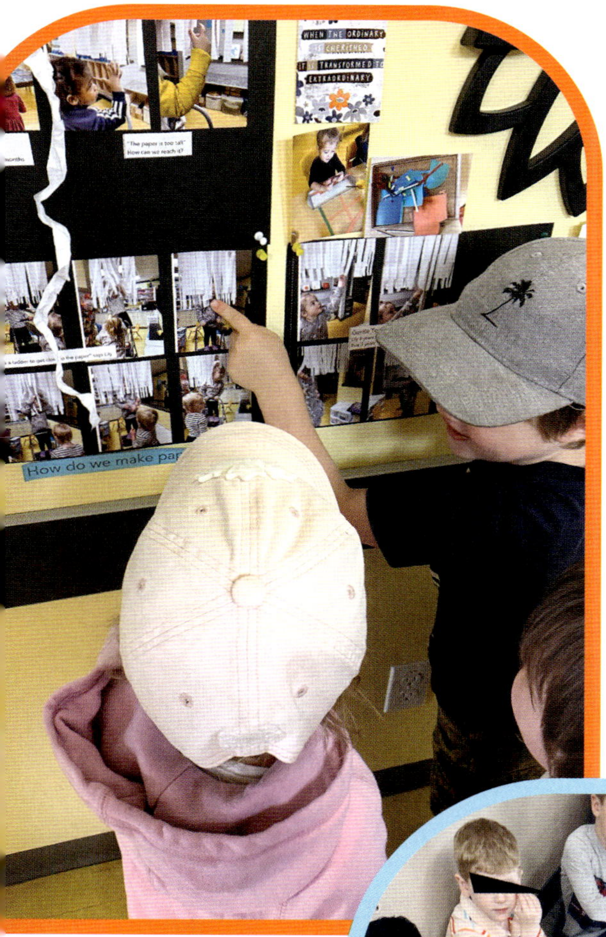

Expression is a sense of making one's own thoughts, ideas, and feelings known. Questions are one of many ways we express ourselves. For young children, magical thinking is a key part of self-expression. As educators, we need to realize that this magical thinking is important work for young children. I feel that we undermine children's thinking by dismissing it as "silly" or "immature" or even by calling it "cute." Instead, we should say, "That is so interesting. I never would have thought of that."

Engagement is a sense of enthusiastic involvement. Asking questions allows children to engage in a classroom's project work. Questions conjure ideas and increase involvement in the children's conversations. I always ask children "What do you think?" when there are a lot of questions about something.

We once had a very large truck pull up to our school's street. The truck dropped a large garbage container and then left. The younger children were at first just fascinated by the large truck and the noise it created, but the older children wanted to know what was in the container and why it had been left on the road. The container was very large, and we could not see into it.

I could have ended the speculation by telling them it was for spring cleanup of trees, branches, and leaves. Instead, I asked, "What do you think is in the container?" One child guessed wild animals, to lots of laughter. Then another child replied that if there were animals in there, we would see the giraffe's head. Others guessed there was garbage in the container. Some wondered whether workers were planning to put stuff in it later. And some thought maybe it was just empty. It was a topic of conversation on our playground all day. Meanwhile, I asked myself whether the event was worthy of a research question and project work.

The next day, the container was gone—and so was the fascination surrounding what was inside the container. I lived in the moment by respecting the children's answers and ideas and by giving them permission to imagine what could be inside the container.

Questions are the foundations of project work. As humans, we are all researchers. We want to know how things work and what will happen next. Children are also researchers, and I think we sometimes forget that in our work. Young children ask *why* all the time—this is a normal stage of development. *Why* questions allow them to take on a vigorous role in their own meaning-making of the world and ultimately their own research. They are trying to figure out how their world works by seeking information and engaging with others. As they ask questions, they develop critical thinking skills.

Children especially ask *why* all the time at about three years old. Loris Malaguzzi tells us that they are not simply asking for an answer from you, but rather they are collecting several possibilities. They are requesting the courage to find the answer. So when a child asks *why*, simply say, "What do you think?"

The types of questions children ask change as they grow and their brains develop. The chart below briefly outlines questions children ask in the first few years of their lives, as I have observed through over forty years of teaching.

Age range	Questions asked
12 months	Pointing and saying "dat." Gesturing and pointing are the main ways babies communicate and ask questions.
20 months to 2 years	An older baby will ask *what* questions and answer simple *where* questions: • The child might point and say, "What's that?" • When asked, "Where is Mommy?" the child says, "Gone."
2 years	A young toddler may answer *where* questions.
2 years to 3 years	An older toddler may ask *who* questions and start to ask *why* and *how* questions. They also start to answer *how* questions. For children this age, educators can start to use *how* questions in research projects, because children can show or tell *how* even with limited language.
3 years to 3½ years	At three years, children may ask *is* questions ("Is Grandpa coming to our house today?") and *do* questions ("Do we go down that street to go home?"). They also more fully understand *how* questions.
3½ years to 4 years old	Preschool children ask *when*, *why*, and *how* questions with confidence.

Play in Action

One fall morning, a group of children was out on the playground. Milo, a four-year-old, looked up and asked me why the moon was still in the sky. I looked up too and said that I didn't know. In my own busy world, it was never something I noticed. Later that day, I looked up online why the moon was in the sky during the day to see what explanation I had missed in my own science education!

The next morning, Milo asked about the moon again. Instead of relaying the scientific information I'd just learned, I simply said, "I see the moon in the sky too. It is so interesting." This questioning went on all week. The other children were starting to notice that the moon was in the sky during the day too.

I believe that it is not my role as an early childhood educator to give children answers; this would interfere in the process they needed to follow to make meaning of their own world. In my role as teacher-researcher, I gather opinions and ideas from all sources, and the children's ideas are the most important.

Milo was never frustrated with me for not answering his questions. Finally, at the end of the week, I asked him, "What do you think?" After a week of thinking, he said, "The moon forgot to go to bed." My mind exploded with joy and excitement as I saw the next step we could take to begin a new project/inquiry-based learning. I'd known in my heart that if I let him think about why the moon was still in the sky during the daytime, he would tell me something wonderful. He trusted me with his magical thinking.

This week of moon gazing helped me believe that if we are patient and if we slow down, we will hear the magic. This was the start of the moon storytelling project. Milo's idea became contagious, and the other children also wanted to tell stories about the moon. The magical story of the moon that forgot to go to bed was the highlight of my year as an educator. The moon became a person. This is often part of magical thinking, as children give inanimate objects personalities and life just like their stuffies or baby dolls.

Storytelling was the verb in this project, and the moon was the vehicle to start the journey. The project was not about the moon or building knowledge and reciting facts about it. The moon instead was a magical being and a fascinating subject for storytelling. It became a person who simply forgot to go to bed.

As I reflect on this time, I know that if I had given Milo the answer I had found online, this magical event never would have happened. This restraint is the foundation for my practice as an early childhood educator: *let children figure out the answers for themselves.*

I also knew that Milo would learn about the moon in school as he got older. I recently saw his mother in town, and she told me that he is still fascinated by the moon as an eleven-year-old. I never answered his original question. Was it important to find the right answer? Did he need the scientific answer?*

*The scientific answer is that the moon and the earth are very close together during certain parts of the year, which allows us to see the moon during the day. The phenomenon is especially prevalent during the glorious harvest moons that happen in the fall.

Questions are at the heart of research and can bring joy to our classrooms. If you look at questions through a lens of magical thinking, then magical experiences will happen in your classroom.

Reflective Questions

How can you incorporate *how* questions into your practice?

How can you use *how* questions to expand your invitations, provocations, and play proposals?

How do you encourage very young children to ask questions and think deeply about their work?

Are you comfortable asking questions for which there are no formal answers?

How can you reframe simple questions like "What color is this?" into *how* questions?

How can you create a classroom environment that values questioning?

How can you use documentation to make your questions visible?

How can you create a *how* question related to your own classroom research this year?

CHAPTER 4

Lisa's Story: Exploring Inquiry-Based Learning with Play Schemas

LISA AGOGLIATI

Schemas help us understand how the child sees, uses, and understands their environment.

Schemas can be a useful starting point in reflecting upon what we are seeing in action.

—**Susan Stacey**

At the beginning of each new school year, when children are learning the names of their teachers and classmates, our faculty intentionally talks about the name of our school. We share with the children and the families that our name, National Child Research Center, is who we are. We are researchers—students and teachers alike—building a unique curriculum path each year based on teachers' observations of the children's play, conversations, interactions with materials, relationships with nature, and outdoor inquiries.

I like to follow Susan Stacey's cycle of inquiry for working with emergent curriculum, which includes five main steps: observing, documenting, raising questions, creating next steps, and providing invitations. Stacey notes:

> When teachers plan without taking time to reflect, something is missing. I call this the missing middle. Rather than following a pattern of observation leading to a response, we can instead strive for a pattern of observation leading to reflection leading to response (2018, 78).

Identifying the children's schemas fits naturally into the first step of observation. When educators consider specific movements of the children's play during the reflection phase (step 3), they may notice that a particular action emerges as an interesting component or a singular focus of the new invitation. When faculty are unsure of the next direction for the curriculum, slowing down the pace of observing and reflecting is critical. I like to call this "simmering with schema."

My experience in the 2020–2021 school year became the ultimate proof for me that sometimes the curriculum can be all about schemas. Shortly after the chalk discovery (see the story in chapter 1 on pages 10–11), I noticed many of my students interacting with art mediums in a transformative way. For example, they were drawing with a handful of crayons and exploring the blending of colors on paper. As I had with the chalk incident, I found myself using the terms *transform* or *transformation* in conversations with children when I observed these schemas leading their play explorations.

At the same time, I had noticed a pattern of *transporting* as a group of several students worked together to move sand from one corner of the sandbox to another and create a pile. Once the pile size was to their satisfaction, they would find new places to start over, transporting the sand again.

Both patterns—*transforming* and *transporting*—were prominent in my observations, so I felt it was time to offer invitations to determine whether one was of more interest to the group than the other. I introduced new materials and questions by sharing with the children how I had noticed them *transforming* and *transporting* recently and was curious about what those words meant to them.

What does *transform* mean?

A butterfly can transform. It changes.

It means you start as something, but then you turn into something else. A butterfly can transform when it gets into its little thing like a cocoon and transforms into a butterfly.

Art can transform. Art can transform into a masterpiece.

A masterpiece is a beautiful thing.

Submarines [can transform]—they can go on land and in water.

Magna-Tiles—I pretended first a house; then I pretended it was a boat.

How can something be *transported* from one place to another?

Humans can be transported on an airplane.

Helicopters can transport.

Hands.

You can transport a car and you can transport a truck.

They could be transported by shovels.

Transport crabs in crab boats.

A squirrel can transport an acorn and might bury it.

Next, we offered opportunities for them to put these new terms into action, using invitations of materials that supported *transforming* and *transporting*. Among the invitations we offered were the following:

- Exploring the effects of evaporation by water painting on reusable calligraphy paper
- Manipulating clay into shapes
- Creating vehicles or structures that could move with wheel pieces from purchased manipulatives (such as Lego, Duplo, or Mobilo building sets)
- Performing a *transporting* "challenge" using building materials and loose parts to create ways to move an object
- Reading featured literature such as *Mossy* by Jan Brett (*transforming*) or *Handa's Surprise* by Eileen Browne (*transporting*)

After two weeks of exploring invitations centered around these two play schemas, I observed that the children showed a consistent preference for materials that echoed *transforming* and a diminished interest in the materials related to *transporting*. Although their engagement was purposeful, I wondered how I could nurture the specific schema exploration beyond simply offering more materials. I felt like I needed (and that the children could benefit from) something to help guide further application and extension of their knowledge about these specific actions.

In searching for something to connect to the children's intention of *transforming*, I reviewed my documentation of the NCRC teaching teams' previous investigations in our early learning, preschool, and prekindergarten classes. I noticed a trend of certain categories—the arts, nature, and connections to community. I now wondered what it would look like to use the observed schema(s) in children's play as a "lens" to examine more deeply the connections between their own *actions* and learning about their world through the exploration of art, nature/science, and the diversity of our community.

It was at this point, with a solid schema direction of *transformation*, that I was ready to try out our first "lens" with the children. Over the next several weeks, the children's responses to discovering this new relationship in their play opened up a rich and meaningful framework within our curriculum.

Transforming in Art

Since art was how this transforming journey had begun, and since it had remained a consistent interest of the children, I decided that art would be our launching point. One of my favorite artists is Mark Bradford. He creates large murals by arranging intricate layers of paper, and then he transforms them further by tearing, making holes, and sanding the surface.

Find Mark Bradford's work on this website:

www.hauserwirth.com/artists/2838-mark-bradford

I introduced my students to Bradford as an artist who *transforms* his materials. We viewed several video clips of Bradford working in his studio with his materials, which included a large collection of paper along with old movie posters, magazines, and newspapers. The children were fascinated, especially with the kiddie pools he had in his studio for soaking the paper before pasting it on the mural. They were excited to try out the transformation process themselves.

As they explored manipulating the paper, our new *transforming* vocabulary emerged, with words like *crumple*, *squeeze*, *rip*, *tear*, *roll*, *fold*, *smooth*, and *scrunch*.

Next, I asked them to brainstorm a list of different types of paper:

- origami paper
- printing paper
- construction paper
- drawing paper
- Post-it Notes
- wrapping paper
- parchment paper
- tissue paper
- book paper

- cardboard
- newspaper

I was able to find many of the items at school, which we used to start building our paper collection. I also invited the children to search at home for paper to bring in. Soon a beautiful palette was constructed in our classroom, including cereal boxes, wrapping paper, origami paper, tissue paper, office paper, greeting cards, and newspaper.

Although we weren't able to bring in a kiddie pool like Bradford used, we did manage to find some large round plastic containers to hold the water-glue mixture, in which we dipped pieces of paper.

After the children finished layering their pieces on a small canvas, we set them aside for several days to dry completely.

We turned to a new video clip of our artist for the next phase of creating our art. Bradford's process with his dried layers of paper and other found materials involves using an electric sander as well as ripping away parts of the solid mound to reveal its layers in a new perspective. With pieces of sandpaper in hand, the children were eager to see what they could discover. They exclaimed with delight, "I see colors!" Their fingers pinched and peeled tiny pieces off the canvas until they were satisfied with what remained.

In deciding how to put together our small individual panels to create the effect of a mural, I invited each child to take a turn arranging their canvas on the floor. I encouraged them to slow down and take a "looking turn" at the other panels before deciding where to place theirs.

After all the pieces were connected, the students voted on how to orient the artwork on the wall, and it was installed in our classroom for the rest of the year.

Transforming in Nature

Nature provokes children into action to formulate their own ideas and self-guided investigations. When children are fully immersed and exposed to experiences with nature, they are being given an open invitation for free adventure. When teachers are guiding young children out into nature—whether it is a large tree-filled playground, a raised garden bed, a small grassy knoll, or a tree box on your school's sidewalk—they are now "nature detectives" searching and unearthing the unknown. Schema or play urges, which may include *gathering/collecting*, *enveloping*, *covering*, *burying*, *trajectory*, or *transforming*, can support curiosity and extend complex play. The more time children spend in nature, the more rooted their experiences become, which allows them to develop recall and store memories. Nature cements the notion for children to investigate and comprehend their natural world.

—*Julie Hunter, NCRC Directing Teacher*

The initial experience with exploring the schema of *transforming* in art demonstrated to me the potential for exploring different relationships with a schema. I decided to move forward and invited the children to think about the lens of *transformation* again, only this time as it related to animals.

What animals do you know that *transform* their body to look different?

Among their responses was a chameleon, which I matched with an invitation to think about animals that use color to transform their bodies. Next, we conducted research as a group by viewing footage of ten different color-changing animals, and then I asked each child which animal they were most interested in learning more about. My plan was to use their responses to determine the order of the animals we would examine, which resulted in the arctic fox as the top choice.

After learning about the seasonal color change of the arctic fox's fur, children began to inquire about other aspects of the animal, such as "How do they play?" and "What do they eat?" I responded, "Is that something you are curious to find out? Is that something we should research?" The resounding cheers and thrusting of hands into the air generated an unexpected pivot to new questions beyond the concept of *transformation*.

- *What do arctic foxes' babies look like?*
- *What do arctic foxes like to play?*
- *How do arctic foxes eat?*
- *What do arctic foxes eat?*
- *How do they catch fish?*
- *How do arctic foxes eat animals bigger than them?*
- *How do they grow so fast?*

Our investigation followed the children's questions. Sometimes that meant providing access to materials for the children to get specific answers to specific questions ("What do arctic foxes eat?"). Other times it meant providing recycled materials so they could transform them into a model of the layers of the arctic tundra. The children answered other questions, such as "What do arctic foxes like to play?" as they dramatized scenarios of arctic foxes playing together after looking at photographs from our research. Since the investigation occurred in the fall when the children were still getting to know each other, acting out situations in which one fox was trying to figure out how to join in the play was helpful in supporting the children's ability to do the same.

Transforming in Our Community and Our World

> Bridging play schemas with diversity, equity, and community allows us to honor the actions of young children and incorporate salient concepts that fall under the diversity umbrella. The beauty of this is that there are so many wonderful resources and ideas, including diverse picture books, that can easily be connected to the various schemas. It requires intentionality and reflection, and I always feel a sense of pride when I can expand the perspective of my students and deepen their appreciation for difference through play.
>
> *—Ashley Nartey, NCRC Director of Diversity, Equity, and Community*

With our original class of twenty-three students separated into three pods during the COVID pandemic, teaching teams were keen to find ways to help the children feel connected as one class community. Letter writing became a big favorite, and my group loved sending pictures and dictating letters about our arctic study to the other cohorts.

During this time, I had also shared with my class a "problem" in the supply closet: a big pile of old, broken, marked-up crayons no one seemed to want to use. We decided to transform them into "new" crayons by peeling all the papers off, sorting them by color, and creating new combinations to be melted together. The result was a mass of more than sixty crayons! They came up with many ideas for what to do with them:

What could we do with our crayons?

Put them in the art studio.

We should hang them on the ceiling to decorate the ceiling.

Let's share some with the other classes.

Take them home to our family.

We can make enough so that everyone can do their idea.

Who should we share these crayons with?

[Children name the other pre-K classes.]

All the classes in NCRC!

There are no other crayons like these.

They're unique.

Yeah, we're all unique.

Their idea to give each child at school a transformed crayon led us to count up the number of children in each class. The children soon realized, though, that we didn't have enough for all the students at NCRC. They had also initially suggested giving the transformed crayons to the all the pre-K classes, so I suggested they figure out how many crayons they would need for those classes. They discovered there were enough to give one crayon to each of the other pre-K students *and* still have some left over for our group to keep in their personal art box. It was a beautiful act of generosity and connection to our pre-K community.

Midyear I approached our diversity director about my experiences with the students using the *transforming* schema as a lens into art and animals. I was curious if she thought diversity could also be used with the lens of exploring *transformation*. She shared with me her experiences in introducing her students to people who have transformed the world through their actions. This idea of connecting the *transforming* schema to our community and our world struck me as very powerful. I had not thought of the schema extending in this way, and our conversation sparked my interest in incorporating this aspect of *transforming* into our curriculum.

As it turned out, an opportunity was approaching by way of the upcoming Martin Luther King Jr. holiday. In my own DEI journey as a white woman of privilege, I often deferred to my coteacher, who is Black, or to the school librarian as the most appropriate educators to discuss Dr. King. So, when the COVID restrictions mandated that small groups be taught by one lead teacher, I had to pause and rethink how I would approach the topic on my own. While my class included diverse cultural backgrounds, such as Persian, Russian, Ukrainian, Chinese, and Korean, none of my students in this small pod were Black.

The Tuesday after the federal holiday, a student mentioned that the day before had been Martin Luther King Jr. Day. I nodded in agreement and listened as he shared what he knew of Dr. King. Looking around our small classroom, my gaze stopped on the large wall display that we'd started during our investigation of Mark Bradford. The display featured photos of him and his work as well as our own Bradford-inspired artwork.

At that moment, I decided to take a risk with the plans for our morning gathering. I started the conversation by pointing out the transformative work of Dr. King, and I referenced the child's earlier comments. Pointing to our display wall, I then shared that if Dr. King had not worked so hard to make sure Black people could do the same things that White people could do, Mark Bradford might not have been able to have his art in a museum for us to see, and we might not have been able to discover this extraordinary artist. As I saw the children's reactions, I felt this recognition of history was genuine and respectful. Most of all, it made a meaningful connection to their journey of learning. I gained from this situation a sense of how play schemas can make DEI concepts, such as inclusion, more concrete for young children as well as deepen children's understanding of and relationship with DEI topics in their own life experiences.

Later in the year, my class learned about peacemakers, specifically women who put their ideas in action at a young age. I found this new perspective of the *transforming* schema resonating again in our discussions of activists such as Greta Thunberg, Malala Yousafzai, and Nzambi Matee.

We also learned about the island of Palau, whose president and first lady turned to local school children for their ideas on what visitors needed to understand about the impact tourism has on the people and the land of Palau. The result was a simple pledge that visitors are required to sign upon arriving in this country. Among its simple and poignant messages includes the phrase, "Act kindly and explore mindfully." Our investigation wrapped up with adding our class and school name to the online pledge to show our support to the people of Palau. Inspired by these stories of children making change, our students reflected on changes they wished to see happen in the world.

Make it so we don't have to wear these masks.

All Black guys would matter.

There are cars [like] solar and electric cars we should use.

People should not take shells or corals from the beaches.

Don't carry trash to the ocean.

Everyone would be healthy. Always.

Our remarkable year of learning together wrapped up with an investigation of the *perspective* schema using light and shadow. There is no doubt that my own perspective on incorporating play schemas into inquiry-based learning experiences was forever changed that year. As we said goodbye at the end of the school year, I was teary-eyed as I took off my mask and, for the first time, offered each child a tender hug. In that moment, I realized that while the year had been filled with the intense challenge of developing meaningful relationships in that unprecedented time, the children had been able to get what they, and I, most needed—to experience true joy together in our learning journey. The year had still been ours to discover. The children had

explored art, nature, their community, and their world. For me, it was proof of the power of play schemas and perseverance, which seem to echo Colleen Wilcox's words, "Teaching is the greatest act of optimism."

See Appendix E for examples of potential investigations of art, nature, and community/world topics connected across specific play schemas.

The following two photo essays show other examples of linking play schemas across investigations.

Aggregating and Perspective

At the beginning of the school year, we noticed the children repeatedly digging holes in the sandbox using shovels or their hands. The sizes varied from very large openings to small holes made by poking a single finger in the sand. Others wanted to make deep holes to contain water. So we used the schema of *aggregating* as our lens into an investigation of holes in nature, such as worm tunnels, chipmunk burrows on our playground, tree cavities, crevices in the ocean, and sinkholes.

After nearly eight weeks of looking into holes, the teaching team thought about how we might consider holes that we look through to view our world differently. We noticed that children were beginning to use the materials in this way by placing two pieces of curved blocks together and looking through the opening. We then shifted to the *perspective* schema to investigate eyeholes used in telescopes, binoculars, kaleidoscopes, and eyewear.

As their interest in holes showed no signs of slowing down, we used the *perspective* schema once more by applying the lens to art. We asked, "How can you create art with holes?" They brainstormed different ways holes can be made in materials, and then we introduced artist Barbara Hepworth, whose sculptures feature a theme of holes. In connection to the round window in our classroom, we also examined the series Of the Land by artist Lou Stovall, which features porthole shapes of seasonal images.

50X/100X 600MM F/12
ASTRONOMICAL TELESCOPE

Enclosing

The children were newly interested in wrapping objects with leaves after seeing one child's discovery on the playground and his demonstration at a whole-group gathering. Soon their engagement with materials expanded to enveloping parts of their bodies or placing materials on a flat object such as a cardboard circle until the space was fully covered. Children also created specific areas of land or water and habitats to enclose related toy animals. We then coupled the lens of *enveloping/enclosing* with nature themes as we explored birds' nests. For example, we learned about the tailorbird, which uses its beak to "sew" leaves together with thin pieces of plants or grass.

When we shifted the lens to examine art with the same schema, we selected artists Christo and Jeanne-Claude, whose work includes breathtaking feats of wrapping fabric around buildings, bridges, and islands. Children explored the process of constructing a building and then selected fabric to enclose their structure. As their inquiry developed around the artists' larger works, we created a short-term art installation on our playground, selecting a recently trimmed tree and working together to completely envelop its remaining trunk and an attached birdhouse.

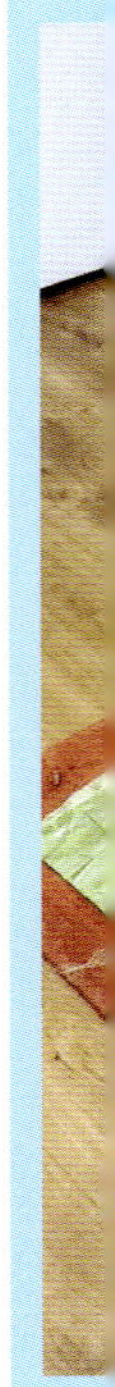

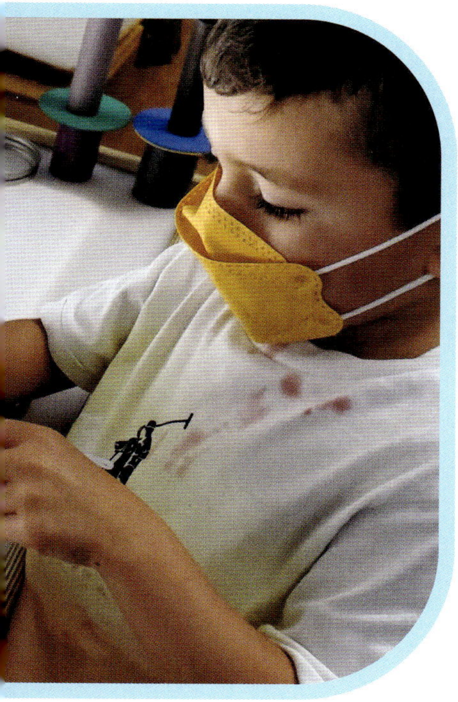

Reflective Questions

What schemas do you notice in the way children create with art materials?

What schemas do you notice in the way children play outside and/or engage with nature (trees, rocks, sticks, sand, and so forth) in your setting?

What schemas can you highlight as you build your class community and recognize diversity in our world?

CHAPTER 5

Heather's Story: Launching Project Work with Play Schemas

HEATHER JACKSON

The child is made of one hundred. The child has a hundred languages, a hundred hands, a hundred thoughts, a hundred ways of thinking of playing, of speaking, a hundred. Always a hundred.

—Loris Malaguzzi

This quote makes me think about the one hundred ways children play and in turn how schemas and verbs are an important part of the one hundred. Verbs and play schemas are part of the life of our school, so I have included several stories from our classrooms to show the full significance of using verbs and play schemas as a planning tool. *Planning, observing, noticing, recording, thinking,* and *wondering* are all verbs. We use these action words every day in our work with children.

The Story of a Mistake

Over the years, I have read *Beautiful Oops* by Barney Saltzberg to children and have loved the message "A spill. A smear. A smudge. A tear. When you *think* you have made a mistake, think of it as an opportunity to make something beautiful!" (2010)

Once upon a time at the Sunflower School, a group of preschool children were researching the question "How does paper transform in water?" In the middle of a table, I placed containers of water with eyedroppers, small pitchers, and tongs. I also supplied cut-up cardboard pieces and crumpled tissue paper in different colors.

At first the children just played with the water, scooping it into cups, using the eyedroppers, and pouring a lot. Then a child gazed at the tissue paper and proceeded to place the balls of crumpled tissue paper on top of the water. The paper slowly sank to the bottom of the container. She stirred the water and tissue paper together. The tissue paper separated into small pieces and floated on top of the water. The child then gathered the tissue paper into a ball and removed it from the water. She manipulated and transformed the paper into a ball. It was like she was playing with clay or playdough. This play lasted for twenty minutes.

The other children watched her transform the tissue paper and then also began adding tissue paper and cardboard to their water containers to see what would happen. They used spoons or punched the cardboard into the water with their hands, then squeezed the water out of the cardboard until it slowly transformed into fibers. The children took out the cardboard and tissue paper mixture and formed it into shapes.

I provided paper towels on the table so the children could lay out their creations. I asked them if they thought the creations would dry or if they would remain wet. The children thought the creations would be wet tomorrow when we returned to school. I wrote down everyone's predictions on

a whiteboard, and then we placed all the paper creations in our art studio. I called them our beautiful oopses, as I had no idea how it would turn out. I did not have an agenda for this work. I simply wanted to see how paper would deteriorate in water.

When we came into school the next day, the children and I were very excited to see that the paper creations were drying and becoming very hard.

We picked them up and tried to manipulate them, but they were too hard. During morning meeting, I brought in the paper creations and asked the children "What do these remind us of?" The children were excited to share their thoughts—C said they looked like paper, F said they looked like balls, N said they still looked wet, and E said they looked like flowers.

When E said they looked like flowers, the other children all agreed and were excited to talk about flowers. During this time, we were also working on our gardens outside and planting seeds, watering, and watching as the plants grew. Spring had arrived, so the gardens in our neighborhood were filled with flowers. I asked, "How could we create flowers in a garden from our paper creations?" Then we read the story *Planting a Rainbow* by Lois Ehlert and figured out that flowers need stems, leaves, roots, and maybe vines. This book helped the children envision the whole flower with stems and leaves.

So the next day, I decided we would create a mural of our paper-creation "flowers." These truly were our beautiful oopses, so we also read that story again. The conversations and drawings were magical. As an educator, I love murals and collaborative art projects. They allow children to work together, build on one idea, and transform a blank piece of paper into something beautiful.

Our study of *transforming* continued with natural materials over the next few weeks. We cut up dried flowers for potion making, and we also continued to add paper to water. This play experience was very exciting for the children even weeks later; indeed, we actively integrated these play proposals into our work until the end of the school year. The children were trying to make meaning of how materials can transform with different mediums, like water, and different tools, like their fingers, scissors, and a mortar and pestle.

We even took some of the leftover beautiful oopses, deconstructed them with our hands, and added water to them. Some of the children transformed the beautiful oopses into flat creations by manipulating the paper with their hands and rolling pins. The beautiful oopses became another sensory material, and I continue to use them regularly in our classrooms.

During our conversations, we often talked about how the paper was transforming into something different. *Transforming* became part of our vocabulary and conversations. We also used a lens of *transforming* as we transformed dirt and water into mud on our playgrounds that summer.

Catching Stars

Once upon a classroom at the Sunflower School, we investigated light and shadows. My teaching partner and I had gathered a few interesting books about the nighttime

sky and stars. We also wanted to look at light and shadows from a different perspective.

Every year, we invite the children to engage with Vincent van Gogh's painting "The Starry Night" for some time; then we host a family event called Starry Night. We make the rooms dark except for fairy lights strung everywhere. Each classroom has many light and shadow experiences for our families to play in. It is an amazing way for families to see our Reggio-inspired practice in a hands-on, experiential way.

During our 2023 Starry Night work, we read *How to Catch a Star* by Oliver Jeffers to catch our children's imaginations. We also read other stories about catching stars or throwing stars back into the sky: *Twinkle* by Nick

Bland, *Stars in a Jar* by Sam Hay, and *I'll Catch You If You Fall* by Mark Sperring.

At one morning meeting, we started talking about how to catch a star and how to transport a star to the sky. The children came up with a list of ideas: *a ladder, a net, a basket, jump into the sky, jump on your bed, my mommy will throw me in the air to catch a star, a rocket ship.* As teacher-researchers, we started thinking about the verb or play schema for these ideas. The verbs we noticed were *catching* and *throwing*, and the play schema was *transporting*. The main research question for our project or inquiry-based learning was "How do you catch and transport a star from the sky?"

I created a web to start our thinking about catching and throwing a star. The children started drawing different ways to catch a star. At the Sunflower School, we love vertical play, so we used the wire of a lampshade to attach and dangle materials like metal stars from the ceiling.

This play went on for two months. We talked about how we could build a ladder and what

materials we would need. We drew blueprints of ladders, built ladders out of wooden craft sticks, and collected stars from families (many former Christmas decorations). The children used wooden blocks to build stairs to climb up to catch a star. We attached photos of the children to blocks so they

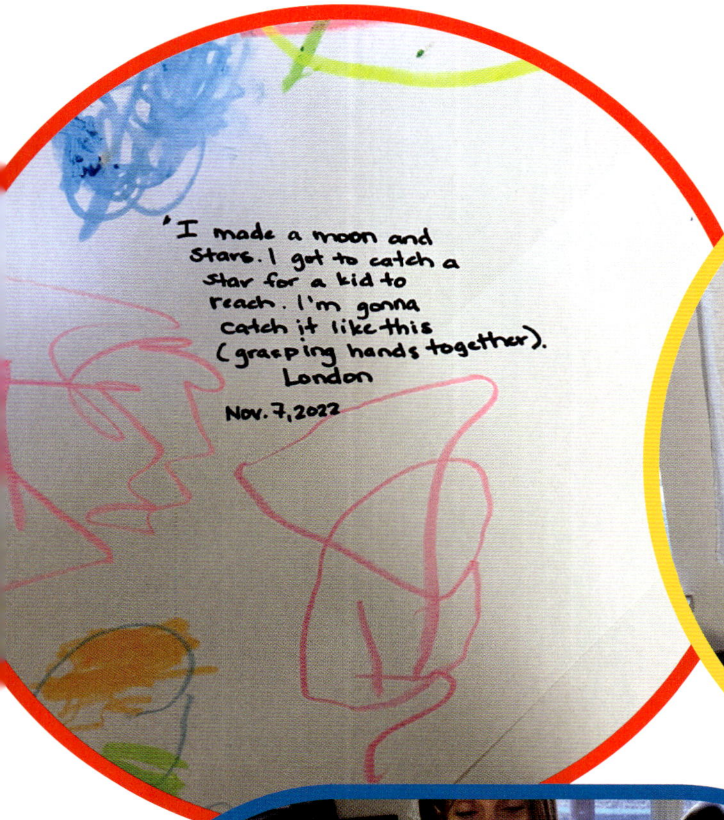
"I made a moon and
stars. I got to catch a
star for a kid to
reach. I'm gonna
catch it like this
(grasping hands together).
London
Nov. 7, 2022

could be part of the play too. Every day, interesting and important work played out as they tried to figure out how to catch a star.

Whale Sharks

One year at the Sunflower School, we happened to begin a whale shark project. This was significant for us as educators because we let the children guide our work. It started when we were investigating Steve Jenkins, an illustrator and children's author. In *Down, Down, Down,* his beautifully illustrated book about oceans, he uses different types of paper to create animals. The page with the whale shark fascinated the children the most. I personally had never heard of whale sharks. They are huge, and they have very large mouths and white dots on their backs. The children loved that the name combines *whale* and *shark* together. The noun of our project was *whale shark,* but we were able to create something more meaningful by using the schema of *transforming* with the verb *moving.*

The enormous mouth was their first discovery. They wanted to watch videos showing whale sharks feeding on fish. It was mesmerizing. The

children repeatedly drew those huge mouths, round and round. We also found out that an adult whale shark has three thousand teeth. One day we asked, "How big do you think the mouth of a whale shark is if it has three thousand teeth?" This began the creation of a life-sized whale shark with a fully functioning mouth.

We soon determined that a whale shark is forty feet long. Each tile on the floor of our classroom is one foot, so we counted the tiles and realized our classroom was too small. Since we concluded that an adult whale shark would be too big in our classroom, one of the children suggested we make a baby whale shark—brilliant!

We talked about which materials to use, how to build the mouth, and how to engineer the body to hang from our ceiling. The children decided the whale shark would be made from cardboard and paper. We gathered cardboard and paper, then created a blueprint of the body and mouth based on photographs and videos. *Down, Down, Down* was a great inspiration for the mouth. We mixed various shades of gray and blue to color the body. The children also created small fish to dangle in front of the whale shark's mouth.

We educators could have researched all the facts about whale sharks ourselves and then regurgitated these facts to the children, but we didn't. Instead, we watched and listened to understand how the children wanted to proceed. When the children asked specific questions about whale sharks, we helped them find the specific answers, whether through online research and videos or by reading nonfiction children's books. As I watched the whale shark come to life, I realized this was the real work of the project: not our teachers' agenda but the children's intentions. I don't think this project would have been so joyful and important if we had followed traditional early childhood themes. The children were empowered to think for themselves and lend their own ideas to this project work.

One child who usually brought lots of stuffies to school suggested we make whale shark stuffies for everyone. I loved that idea, so we talked about how we could make them. We asked what materials we would need, how we would start, whether we could sew them ourselves, and many more

questions. I sew a bit, so I became the expert for this part of the project. I had the children each draw a whale shark, and we created patterns from their drawings. I helped the children pin the patterns onto the material, cut them out, and then sew the pieces together. Once we finished sewing, I showed the children how to stuff their whale sharks.

The power that I helped these children cultivate was enormous. They learned how to sew, measure, count, safely use tools like very sharp sewing needles and sewing scissors, and work collaboratively. One child was so excited when he finished sewing his whale shark that he proudly yelled, "I did it myself!"

Years later, one of the children brought me a plastic whale shark he had found at a local dollar store. He gave it to me with a card thanking me for the whale shark project. His mother told me that he still has the whale shark stuffie in his room. Every time I see a whale shark, the universe tells me that this was an important part of my life as an educator and an important part of the children's lives.

Spirals

Once upon a time at the Sunflower School, I was outside with a group of preschoolers, watching them build with stones in an attempt to capture ants. The children were very frustrated as the ants escaped. One of them asked how we could keep bugs inside a "house." When I posed the question to the large group, they had many ideas, including putting a roof on the house and making the walls bigger and taller.

One two-and-a-half-year-old boy kept saying we should make it in "circles." He said it three times before I understood what he was saying. I asked him to show us his ideas. He took the chalk and drew circles and more circles until they became swirls and spirals. I then helped draw a giant spiral on our playground as a guide, and some of the children added stones and other natural materials on top of the line. When we were finished, we had a giant spiral of stones, pine cones, and sticks. The ants were happy to stay inside the spiral and crawl around and around.

The play schema in this story is *transforming*. The children transformed the chalk spiral into a natural materials spiral. They also transformed the stone and pebble house into a spiral that would contain the ants. The schema of *enveloping* also holds a lot of potential for this play. How can we transform other natural materials into something that will envelop insects?

This spiral was constant in our playground that summer. The children protected it and added ladybugs, worms, and ants. The little boy who had come up with the "circles" idea was proud of the spiral all summer. Had I not listened to him, this experience may not have happened, or it might have been simplistic rather than fully realized. I was open to what the children were thinking, and my mind was in a state of flow as I watched and participated. The collaborative work of the children was interesting and so engaging. The photos speak for themselves.

Hunting and Gathering Metal and More

Once upon a springtime at the Sunflower School, a preschool class was investigating metal as part of a bigger schoolwide materials project. Metal was a new material for many of our educators and children. During the morning meeting time, I asked the children what they knew about metal. I also had a basket of metal objects for the children to touch, examine their properties, and start talking about metal. It was not my place to fill their heads with many facts about metal. I always want the children to form their own ideas about materials. We recorded the children's answers and conversations so we could review them during our planning times. We also asked parents for donations of metal pieces.

During any investigation, I look for children's books to spark our imaginations and relaunch our ideas. I found *More* by I. C. Springman and illustrated by Brian Lies. I was drawn to this book because of the realistic and colorful illustrations. The story is about a magpie hunting and gathering shiny metal pieces and placing them in its nest. A mouse told the magpie that there were too many metal pieces in the nest and that the branch would break. I did a little research of my own and found out that magpies do collect shiny objects for their nests. They are hoarders. The children loved this story and asked for it to be read every day.

Children worldwide ask for stories to be reread as they try to make meaning. We educators can help with this experience by providing them with pieces of the story to reenact. Then the children create their own stories with the characters.

My teaching partner and I wanted to expand and enrich this story for our children's play. We created a web of the story, highlighting the verbs *hunting* and *gathering*, and we documented and recorded the children's amazing ideas in our journals. This documentation was an important part of the project, as it ensured that we would not forget any of our children's thoughts.

Then we looked at the story again and asked, "What objects do you notice in the story?"

We started to collect a list:

- branch
- birds
- mice
- shiny objects
- metal objects
- old keys
- shiny jewelry
- My grandpa has those round things (washers).
- nest

The list was full of great materials, so my teaching partner and I started collecting some of these items to share with the children. We asked families to send in found objects too.

One of the children thought we needed a branch to display our objects. The children wanted to figure out how to attach the materials onto a branch without the branch falling. They realized that if they attached too many materials to one spot of the branch that the branch could fall as it was too heavy. So we went on a hunting and gathering journey outside that week, and we found a branch that was perfect for our story. It would form a base for displaying the items we collected.

We decided to hang it from the ceiling because, as one child explained, a real branch is in the air. We hung it high enough so that it would not be in the way of other play and movement around the room. But then our next question was "How can we hang shiny objects on the branch if we can't reach it?"

One child told us a ladder would help. We had a portable stepladder in the school that was the perfect size for the children to climb up and down safely.

The children discussed the safety of the ladder at length, as they found this new addition to their play interesting but a bit scary. One child told us that only one person could climb at a time because it was very dangerous. "We can't jump on the ladder—that's also dangerous," they said. We thought maybe they had some previous experience with dangerous ladders.

Once all the safety measures were in place, the children took turns climbing the ladder so they could begin attaching and dangling the shiny objects. Children helped one another—one child would stand on the ladder and ask for materials, and the others would gather them. We added some metal hooks to the branch, and we hooked a clothespin bag onto the ladder. The bag gave the children easy access to the metal materials and additional fastenings. The ladder was such a great idea for incorporating a little risky play indoors that we have kept it as a permanent fixture.

This play was a highlight for about two months. It supported our intention of *hunting* and *gathering* while also becoming a beautiful collaborative play experience. We also added other enrichments, including light and shadow play. We placed a work light on the floor near the branch so the materials could shine and reflect light onto the wall. The children could see the shadows and the reflective properties of the shiny materials. We also added the characters in printouts from the book to this play, as they were so vivid in the story.

This investigation supported many of the intentions of our classroom:

- Supporting our verbs of *hunting* and *gathering* (going on treasure hunts around our school to find shiny objects and asking for donations from home)
- Offering interesting and important materials (metal) and combining materials like light and shadow play with dangling and attaching
- Increasing parent engagement (donations of metal and shiny objects)
- Introducing important and engaging children's literature (*More* by I. C. Springman)
- Supporting collaboration of children in play (which supports belonging)
- And most important, increasing joy, which cultivates well-being

The Transformation and Decay of Pumpkin Jack

Once upon an autumn at the Sunflower School, we read *Pumpkin Jack* by Will Hubbell. In this story, a pumpkin seed grows into a pumpkin and becomes a jack-o'-lantern. Then a boy takes the pumpkin into the forest for the animals to eat over the winter. We have read this story repeatedly to our children over the years. They love the illustrations, and so do I.

At the end of October, we and the children gathered the pumpkins from our school gardens, cut them up into pieces, and transported them to the forest.

Once we deposited the pumpkins into the forest, we thought about how *Pumpkin Jack* started at the beginning, with a pumpkin seed. Our ideas began to grow. Soon we decided on several experiences: once a week over the fall and winter, we would come to see what was happening to our pumpkins, and in the spring we would look for evidence of our pumpkins and seeds.

During our winter visits, we asked the children to wonder what was happening to the pumpkins in the forest. "All the animals will have full bellies," said one child. She was very satisfied with that answer and felt a sense of security that the animals would not be hungry.

In the spring, we thought about *Pumpkin Jack* again as we planted pumpkin seeds in our school gardens. Our questions to the children were "How does a seed change into a plant?" and "How can we draw the inside of a pumpkin seed?" and "How will our pumpkins look once they've grown?" We also journeyed often to the forest and found what we thought were

pumpkin leaves. "They look the same as our pumpkins at school," said one child.

The following fall, we ventured into the forest to see if we were growing pumpkins. Unfortunately, we did not find any pumpkins. Some of the children were concerned that someone had taken the pumpkins from the forest. We had hoped the cycle would begin again in the spring, with a new patch of pumpkins, but unfortunately it didn't—a real-life lesson in how nature works.

The verb *transforming* is the center of our investigation. The charm of decay is in *transforming*. How can a jack-o'-lantern transform into food for animals? How can a pumpkin seed transform into a plant? How can decay become beautiful?

These stories illustrate our use of verbs and play schemas as the central idea for our project work and play-based learning. The webs shared here show how educators' research work and children's meaning-making can be enriched and expanded. The *how* questions sprinkled throughout these stories help expand on new ideas about the verbs and play schemas. The stories are also paired with good children's literature, because stories with compelling plots and interesting characters draw children's attention and intentions. The characters become part of our projects and play-based learning. How can you transform a children's book into a project or play-based learning? This is a great staff meeting idea.

Reflective Questions

How can you use a children's book to highlight a verb or play schema?

What favorite children's book could you use to create a project using the play schema presented in it?

How can you provide play proposals to support a favorite story in your classroom?

CONCLUSION

A Play Tapestry

Fabric can only be made with warp and weft. It doesn't work with only one thread, rather the two threads act in a symbiotic relationship, giving and taking from the other, coming together to create something meaningful.

—Nate Vaughn

As we return to the image of weaving, the symbiotic relationship between play schemas and curriculum sparks us to reflect on the value of schema play for ourselves as educators and our students as learners. Whether the format is emergent, project-based, flexible framework, or published, the curriculum's ability to nurture and grow authentic connections to children's inquiry depends on educators' willingness to respond to the play schemas that appear naturally.

While the curriculum often carries our children to learning about people, places, or things, play schemas evoke an action-based construction of knowledge. Incorporating observed play schemas directly from the children promotes a kinesthetic form of inquiry, and it fosters complex, genuine, and rich curriculum experiences for both teachers and students. Through our reflections and responses as educators, we can create opportunities to launch and relaunch our children's learning with these actions of play. Above all, we can create these opportunities when we give children time to play.

Among the many connections we authors discovered as we collaborated on this book was the importance of valuing schemas through the words of the children. Their organic vocabulary often elevates the name of the action to a new level of comprehension for students and teachers alike. For example, as the NCRC pre-K students began to add daily contributions to their Enclosing Word Wall, one that struck Lisa was the simple yet accurate description of *enclosing* as "put stuff around other stuff." Another time, a group of three- and four-year-olds explained to Lisa that they needed to use the paintbrush to "*push* the paint on the paper." By using children's action words, we honor their natural ability to discover, explore, and name play schemas.

To honor the way children use their words to share their magical thinking and world of possibilities, Heather remembers many favorite moments:

"I am trying to *focustrate*," said Eliza.

"Are you ready to play?" said Mya to the funnel.

"Heather, that's not important—*this* is important. My drawing is important," said Olivia.

"That's just silly. *This* is the real life," said Ella about her work designing with loose parts.

"The dandelions look like they are at a party," said Eliza.

"Are you ready for a ride?" Tessa asked her paintbrush and paint.

"Can we stop talking so that I can do something interesting?" asked Ella.

"You have to blow the wish away so that it will come true," said Marcus as he blew on the dandelion.

"Don't worry—we always do something magical," said Eliza when her mom asked what we would do at school that day.

Eliza was a prolific thinker for the two years she was in my class. I was always fascinated by and thankful for her thoughts and ideas. I listened.

We invite you to consider the following ideas as you move forward with your own journey using play schemas as a part of your inquiry-based learning and project work:

- Ground your understanding of play schemas by reading through the work of Nadia Jaboneta and Deb Curtis.
- Extend your work with young children by reflecting on the actions that appear in children's play and considering corresponding schema categories.
- Incorporate the language of schemas into your class discussions, presentation of new materials, and conversations with children.
- Deepen your work with play schemas by responding to observed play schemas through the lens of the following:
    - Visual and performing arts
    - Nature and science
    - Community and world connections
    - Social-emotional learning
- Document and share your work with play schemas and curriculum with others.

Lisa's Closing Thoughts

The 2020–2021 school year unfolded like no other year in my entire teaching career. It was transformative. Ever since, I've found myself eagerly approaching each new school year, excited to see what schemas the children will bring to us to shape our learning journey. I have come to relish the moments of discovering, naming, and playing with schemas inside and outside the classroom. Once schemas become visible to us and our children, it seems that they are everywhere around us!

I am deeply thankful to all my students, whose boundless questions and love of research helped my work with emergent curriculum flourish. In trying to describe my experience of transformation as a teacher, I turn to words from a student in my little pod back in 2020 on what transforming meant to her:

It means you start as something and then bloom.

Heather's Closing Thoughts

Our work with children is alive, engaging, and full of verbs. This school year, as I have been writing this book, verbs have been very evident to me. Once I took the threads of verbs and play schemas and wove them together with my knowledge and experience of the Reggio-inspired approach, I felt very joyful and happy in my work.

I think back to Loris Malaguzzi's inspiring words: "Ideas fly, bounce around, accumulate, rise, fall apart and spread until one of them takes a decisive hold and flies higher and conquers the entire group." I hope that our book has taken hold of your heart and thinking. We hope that you now have a new way of thinking about early childhood education and that you begin to weave verbs and play schemas into your work as you observe your children's actions of play.

Appendix A

Analysis of the Play in Action

The chart on the following pages can help uncover the real work of a project through the lens of a verb or play schemas.

Date:	Program:	Ages of Children:
Observations of the Play: What do you notice? What does it remind you of?		
What catches your curiosity as the children play?		
What captivates you as you watch and listen to play?		
What is interesting and important about this play?		
What fascinates the children?		

What are they trying to accomplish?			
Essences of the play	**Play schemas you have noticed**	**Verbs that describe the essences of the play**	**Enriching the play**

Actual Observation from the Sunflower School

Date: *October 2023* **Program:** *Preschool* **Ages of Children:** *3-year-olds*

Observations of the Play: What do you notice? What does it remind you of?

In the morning on the preschool playground, a group of 5 preschoolers started gathering and carrying crates to the boat [wooden boat for dramatic play]. They worked together almost silently to fill the boat with crates. Once the boat was full of crates, they began to climb over the crates and walk on top of them. At this point, there were about 10 children playing. This looked a bit risky to me. I moved in closer to hear the conversation, and they were talking about climbing and helping one another climb to the top of the crates. This continued for 20 minutes, and then they left. This play happened every day for a month.

What catches your curiosity as the children play?

There were no conversations during the transporting of the crates. They just knew that they needed to fill the boat.

What captivates you as you watch and listen to play?

They collaborated to help one another. No one fell or got hurt during the climbing.

What is interesting and important about this play?

They silently collaborated. These children have been together since they were toddlers. They know one another and can work together.

What fascinates the children?

The transporting of the crates. Then the climbing on the crates. The risky play is fascinating.

What are they trying to accomplish?			
They are transporting the crates to make a very large pile to climb together.			
Essences of the play	**Play schemas you have noticed**	**Verbs that describe the essences of the play**	**Enriching the play**
Togetherness in transporting	*Transporting*	*Transporting together*	*How can we carry the crates differently?*
Sense of belonging	*Transforming crates into a pile*		*How can we move the crates differently?*
Risky/adventurous play			*How might we add a pulley system?*
			Can we use wagons, wheelbarrows?
			How can we as educators feel safe about this play?

Appendix B

Play Schema Brainstorm Sheet

Current Curriculum Study/Topic/Exploration/Investigation
What are the neutral or open-ended materials currently available to the children?

What prominent play schemas match the actions of the children's play with neutral or open-ended materials?

Combining and/or changing materials
[Transforming]

Making materials or their bodies move in a certain way
[Trajectory]

Joining together/taking apart materials
[Connecting/Disconnecting]

Creating layers with materials
[Aggregating]

Engaging with materials to roll, turn, spin
[Rotation/Circularity]

Moving objects from one place to another
[Transporting]

Wrapping things up with materials or building with emphasis on what is inside
[Enclosing/Enveloping]

Turning materials around to see from different angles or looking through or under items
[Orientation/Perspective]

Manipulating materials to go through a boundary and out the other side
[Going through a boundary]

Placing or arranging materials in a particular way/pattern
[Ordering/Positioning]

How can the identified play schemas be used to make a connection to a new aspect of the study?

____

____

____

____

____

____

Example: A class is studying the ocean, and the teachers notice *trajectory* schema in the children's play with neutral materials. Teachers can connect the observed *trajectory* play schema to new ocean invitations to explore the movement of waves, currents, or the path of an animal's movement while diving into or coming out of the ocean.

Appendix C

Play Schema as a Transition Tool within Flexible Curriculum Framework *

*Example illustrated with the Creative Curriculum

Theme Progression	**Schema Category**	**Schema Connections with Thematic Content**
First Six Weeks Study → Tubes and Tunnels Study	*Transporting*	First Six Weeks Study *Transporting to school/home* *Transportation in our community*
Tubes and Tunnels Study → Light Study	*Moving through a Boundary* *Trajectory*	Tubes and Tunnels Study Effects of water and air moving through tubes at different speeds The use of tubes and tunnels in our community (e.g., bank tubes or vehicular tunnels)
Light Study → Clothing Study	*Perspective/ Orientation*	Light Study Shadow investigation and effects of different positions of objects blocking sun
Clothing Study → Exercise Study	*Enclosing/ Enveloping*	Clothing Study How special clothing envelops the body for protection (e.g., for firefighters, surgeons)

	Schema Connections with Thematic Content and Transition to New Study	Schema Connections with Play in the Classroom
	Tubes and Tunnels Study What can tubes and tunnels transport? Where are tubes and tunnels used for transporting in our community?	Materials available for play that support theme and invite schema exploration with *transporting*
	Light Study How does light move through a boundary? What shape is the light when it projects across the room? How does the path of light change when it reflects or refracts?	Materials available for play that support theme and invite schema exploration with *moving through a boundary* or *trajectory*
	Clothing Study When you place this large piece of fabric on your waist, what kind of clothing does it remind you of? When you place the fabric over your shoulders, you could be wearing a ___________.	Materials available for play that support theme and invite schema exploration with *perspective/orientation*
	Exercise Study If you covered your head with this cap and covered your eyes with these goggles, what kind of exercise would you be doing? If you covered your head with this helmet, what kind of exercise would you be doing?	Materials available for play that support theme and invite schema exploration with *enclosing/enveloping*

Appendix D

Play Schema as a Transition Tool within Structured Thematic-Based Curriculum * *Example illustrated with Frog Street curriculum		
Theme Progression	**Schema Category**	**Schema Connections with Thematic Content**
Awesome Me → My Family and Friends	*Connecting*	Awesome Me Physical Me—Body part connections Feeling Me—Heart-mind well-being Social Me—Discover common interests Curious Me—How things work
My Family and Friends → Color, Shape, and Size	*Positioning/ Ordering*	My Family and Friends Immediate Family—Sort by hair or eye color. Sort by age, youngest to oldest. My Relatives—Map of your family My Community—Who uses a vehicle to do their job in my neighborhood? Who uses a building? Sort the ways we travel to school.
Color, Shape and Size → Safe and Healthy Me	*Enclosing/ Enveloping*	Color, Shape, and Size Color—What happens when you cover yellow with blue? Shape—Looking at shapes "inside" shapes (e.g., concentric rings or two triangles to form a diamond) Size: Matryoshka dolls

	Schema Connections with Thematic Content and Transition to New Study	Schema Connections with Play in the Classroom
	My Family and Friends Immediate Family—Who lives with you at home? Similarities to other peers My Relatives—How do/can you stay connected to people in your family who live in other places? My Community—What people do you see in your community who look like you? How do their jobs connect to you?	Materials available for play that support theme and invite schema exploration with *connecting*
	Color, Shape, and Size Color—Order of the rainbow, sets of primary/secondary colors, colors arranged from dark to light Shape—Arrangement of shapes to create images of houses, animals, or people Size—Taking photos of buildings in the school neighborhood and sorting by tallest to shortest	Materials available for play that support theme and invite schema exploration with *positioning/ordering*
	Safe and Healthy Me Safe Me—A seat belt that keeps your body safely inside the car, a bike helmet that encloses your entire head, a crosswalk that creates a safe space to walk across the street Healthy Me—What is on the outside of your body to keep you healthy and safe? What is on the inside? Eating Well—What foods are enclosed in something we need to remove before we eat them? [e.g., banana, avocado] Active Me—Moving inside a Hula-Hoop	Materials available for play that support theme and invite schema exploration with enclosing/enveloping

Appendix E

Resources for Pairing Play Schemas with Art, Nature, and Community

CREATED BY LISA AGOGLIATI, JULIE HUNTER, AND ASHLEY NARTEY

Schema	Play Schemas and Visual/Performing Arts	
	Topics	**Resources**
Transporting	Dance: How dancers travel in space Artists inspired by transportation	Pilobolus Dance Company https://www.youtube.com/watch?v=iGKa4Albtsl&list=PLfLpFsUtJnOazvZPnn9T7ZVUnCCGZDFtD&index=3 Transportation in works of art https://www.nga.gov/learn/teachers/lessons-activities/uncovering-america/transportation.html
Transforming	Tyree Guyton Anna Atkins	*Magic Trash: A Story of Tyree Guyton and His Art* by J. H. Shapiro *The Bluest of Blues: Anna Atkins and the First Book of Photographs* by Fiona Robinson

	Play Schemas and Nature		Play Schemas and Our Community/World	
	Topics	**Resources**	**Topics**	**Resources**
	How animals carry their babies How animals carry food to their homes	*Carry Me! Animal Babies on the Move* by Susan Stockdale *Chipmunk Secrets: Fiston, the Funny Little Chipmunk, Shows You Their Secrets!* by Lieve Snellings	Diversity – different ways people carry things & travel Immigration Inclusion	*Carry Me* by Rena D. Grossman *Dreamers* by Yuyi Morales *The Girl Who Figured It Out: The Inspiring True Story of Wheelchair Athlete Minda Dentler Becoming an Ironman World Champion* by Minda Dentler
	Color changing animals Animal Metamorphosis	*National Geographic: Animals That Change Color* by Libby Romero Ladybugs, Butterflies, Bees, Beetles, Moths	People who have transformed the world through their actions	*Martin's Big Words* by Doreen Rappaport *Malala's Magic Pencil* by Malala Yousafzai *Greta and the Giants* by Zoë Tucker *Magic* by Mirelle Ortega *We Are Water Protectors* by Carole Lindstrom

Schema	Play Schemas and Visual/Performing Arts	
	Topics	**Resources**
Connecting/Disconnecting	Romare Bearden	*My Hands Sing the Blues: Romare Bearden's Childhood Journey* by Jeanne Walker Harvey
	Jean-Michel Basquiat	*Radiant Child: The Story of Young Artist Jean-Michel Basquiat* by Javaka Steptoe
Rotation/Circularity	Yayoi Kusama	*Yayoi Kusama: From Here to Infinity* by Sarah Suzuki
	Alma Thomas	*Ablaze with Color: A Story of Painter Alma Thomas* by Jeanne Walker Harvey
	Alice Sheppard	*I Will Dance* by Nancy Bo Flood

Play Schemas and Nature		Play Schemas and Our Community/World	
Topics	**Resources**	**Topics**	**Resources**
Unique animal friendships	*Owen and Mzee: The True Story of a Remarkable Friendship* told by Isabella Hatkoff, Craig Hatkoff, and Paula Kahumbu	Belonging	*Strictly No Elephants* by Lisa Mantchev *Neither* by Airlie Anderson *A Friend for Henry* by Jenn Bailey
Animal symbiosis	*How to Clean a Hippopotamus: A Look at Unusual Animal Partnerships* by Steve Jenkins and Robin Page *Animal Sidekicks: Amazing Stories of Symbiosis in Animals and Plants* by Macken Murphy	Family constellations	*Stella Brings the Family* by Miriam B. Schiffer *I Love Us! A Book About Family* by Clarion Books
		Friendship	*A Book of Bridges: Here to There and Me to You* by Cheryl Keely
Animal Behaviors	*Line Up! Animals in Remarkable Rows* by Susan Stockdale	Diversity in our world	*This is How We Do It: One Day in the Lives of Seven Kids from around the World* by Matt Lamothe
Spirals in nature	*Swirl by Swirl* by Joyce Kidman	Inclusion	*Meeting Mimi: A Story About Different Abilities* by Francie Dolan
Dung beetles	*Steve the Dung Beetle: On a Roll* by Susan R. Stolz	Family Holidays	*Let's Celebrate!* by Kate DePalma
		Birthdays	*Birthdays Around the World* by Margriet Ruurs

Schema	Play Schemas and Visual/Performing Arts		
	Topics	**Resources**	
Enclosing/Enveloping	Maya Lin	*Maya Lin: Artist-Architect of Light and Lines* by Jeanne Walker Harvey	
	Christo and Jeanne Claude	*Christo and Jeanne-Claude* by Jacob Baal-Teshuva	
	Matryoshka doll art	*Masha and Her Sisters* by Suzy Ultman	
	Ruth Asawa	*A Life Made by Hand: The Story of Ruth Asawa* by Andrea D'Aquino	
	Isamu Noguchi	*A Boy Named Isamu* by James Yang	
	Jordan Baker-Caldwell	https://jordancanfly.com/	

Play Schemas and Nature	
Topics	**Resources**
Marsupials	*About Marsupials: A Guide for Children* by Cathryn Sill and John Sill *What Do You Know about Animals with Pouches?* by Francine Topacio
Birds that make spherical or dome nests	*A Nest Is Noisy* by Dianna Hutts Aston *Mama Built a Little Nest* by Jennifer Ward
Animals that live in dens, burrows, or caves	*Animal Homes* by Mary Holland *Home Sweet Burrow* by Mary Elizabeth Salzmann *Home Sweet Cave* by Mary Elizabeth Salzmann
Animals that enclose with their bodies	*Trapdoor Spiders* by Claire Archer *Parrotfish* by Cari Meister
Animals that live in shells	*Armadillo Antics* by Bill Martin, Jr. and Michael Sampson *Herman the Hermit Crab* by Cindy W. Hollingsworth

Play Schemas and Our Community/World	
Topics	**Resources**
Foods across cultures	*Dumpling Day* by Meera Sriram
Cultural traditions, clothing, & artifacts	*Nesting Dolls* by Vanessa Brantley-Newton *A Garland of Henna* by Varsha Bajaj *The Many Colors of Harpreet Singh* by Supriya Kelkar *The Proudest Blue: A Story of Hijab and Family* by Ibtihaj Muhammad and S.K. Ali
Socio-economic status	*Maddi's Fridge* by Lois Brandt *Saturday at the Food Pantry* by Dianne O'Neill *A Chair for My Mother* by Vera B. Williams
Different abilities/ Inclusion	*The Big Umbrella* by Amy June Bates *Emmanuel's Dream: The True Story of Emmanuel Ofosu Yeboah* by Laurie Ann Thompson *The Circles All Around Us* by Brad Montague

Schema	Play Schemas and Visual/Performing Arts	
	Topics	Resources
Orientation/Perspective	Yayoi Kusama	*Yayoi Kusama: Infinity Mirrors* by Mika Yoshitake
	Zaha Hadid	*The World Is Not a Rectangle: A Portrait of Architect Zaha Hadid* by Jeanette Winter
	Frida Kahlo	*Frida Kahlo and Her Animalitos* by Monica Brown
	Isamu Noguchi	*A Boy Named Isamu* by James Yang
	Julie Mehretu	https://www.widewalls.ch/artists/julie-mehretu
	Barbara Hepworth	*Barbara Hepworth What Do You See?* by Laura Carlin
	Lou Stovall	*Of the Land: The Art and Poetry of Lou Stovall* edited by Will Stovall
Ordering/Positioning	Faith Ringgold	*Faith Ringgold: Narrating the World in Pattern and Color* by Sharna Jackson
	Kumi Yamashita	http://kumiyamashita.com/light-shadow
	Alma Thomas	*Ablaze with Color: A Story of Painter Alma Thomas* by Jeanne Walker Harvey

Play Schemas and Nature		Play Schemas and Our Community/World	
Topics	**Resources**	**Topics**	**Resources**
Nature in your community	*Outside Your Window: A First Book of Nature* by Nicola Davies *Outside In* by Deborah Underwood	Points of view	*Outside My Window* by Linda Ashman *Another* by Christian Robinson *We Disagree* by Bethanie Deeney Murguia *Same, Same but Different* by Jenny Sue Kostecki-Shaw *The Shape of Home* by Rashin Kheiriyeh
Endangered animals	*Don't Let Them Disappear: 12 Endangered Species Across the Globe* by Chelsea Clinton		
Unique animals	*Pipsqueaks, Slowpokes, and Stinkers: Celebrating Animal Underdogs* by Melissa Stewart		
Space perspective	*A Tiny Brown Monkey on the Big Blue Earth* by Tory Christie	Different abilities	*You are Enough: A book about Inclusion* by Margaret O'Hair
		Kindness/empathy	*The Rabbit Listened* by Cori Doerrfeld *The Invisible Boy* by Trudy Ludwig
Trees	*Just Like Me, Climbing a Tree: Trees around the World* by Durga Yael Bernhard	Race/ethnicity	*All the Colors We Are* by Katie Kissinger
Symmetry	*Seeing Symmetry* by Loreen Leedy	Diversity in our world	*Eyes That Kiss in the Corners* by Joanna Ho *Becoming Vanessa* by Vanessa Brantley-Newton
Animals that move in lines	*Line Up! Animals in Remarkable Rows* by Susan Stockdale		
		Gender identity	*Julián Is a Mermaid* by Jessica Love

Schema	Play Schemas and Visual/Performing Arts	
	Topics	**Resources**
Trajectory	Jackson Pollock	*Action Jackson* by Jan Greenberg *Art* by Patrick McDonnell
	Bill Taylor	*It Jes' Happened: When Bill Taylor Started to Draw* by Don Tate
	Kinetic sculpture	https://www.thecoolist.com/incredible-kinetic-sculptures/Action Painting
	Firework displays	*A Year of Celebrations* by Carrie Lara
Aggregating	Jacob Lawrence	*Jake Makes a World: Jacob Lawrence, A Young Artist in Harlem* by Sharifa Rhodes-Pitts
	Faith Ringgold	*Faith Ringgold: Narrating the World in Pattern and Color* by Sharna Jackson
	Alma Thomas	*Ablaze with Color: A Story of Painter Alma Thomas* by Jeanne Walker Harvey
Moving Through a Boundary	Ghost net textile artists	https://www.youtube.com/watch?v=oUVlDGauaol
	Tin punch art	https://www.vandykes.com/blog/hardware-blogs/the-art-of-tin-punching/b/the-art-of-tin-punching/
	Weaving	Artist Joyce J. Scott *Rainbow Weaver* by Linda Elovitz Marshall

Play Schemas and Nature		Play Schemas and Our Community/World	
Topics	**Resources**	**Topics**	**Resources**
Animal tongues	*What If You Had an Animal Tongue!?* by Sandra Markle	Activism in our community	*I Am One: A Book of Action* by Susan Verde
American dippers	American Bird Conservancy: https://abcbirds.org/bird/american-dipper/	Standing up/speaking out	*Say Something!* by Peter H. Reynolds
Mudskippers	Mudskippers: The Fish That Walk on Land BBC Earth video https://www.youtube.com/watch?v=CAQuoH_fOWM	Kindness/empathy	*If You Plant a Seed* by Kadir Nelson *Be Kind* by Pat Zietlow Miller *I Walk with Vanessa* by Kerascoët
Flying squirrels	*The Fantastic Flying Squirrel* by Nic Bishop	Immigration/Emigration	*A Place to Grow* by Soyung Pak
Male seahorses	*Mister Seahorse* by Eric Carle		
Wildebeest Migration	https://education.nationalgeographic.org/resource/natures-most-impressive-animal-migrations/	Activism	*Sometimes People March* by Tessa Allen *We Are Water Protectors* by Carole Lindstrom
Red Crab Migration	https://parksaustralia.gov.au/christmas/discover/nature/animals/red-crab/		
Sociable Weaver Birds communal nest	https://www.youtube.com/watch?v=62G9kw9Ziek		
Tailor Birds	https://www.youtube.com/watch?v=QQMYpzbQIDA	Diversity in home entrances and cultural traditions for welcoming visitors or entering a home	*Home* by Carson Ellis *If You Lived Here* by Giles Larouche
Wildlife crossings	*Make Way for Animals! A World of Wildlife Crossings* by Meeg Pincus		

Appendix F

Play Schema Connections to Social-Emotional Learning Concepts

Social-emotional learning (SEL) competencies put forth by the Collaborative for Academic, Social, and Emotional Learning (CASEL)	**Self-awareness:** The ability to accurately recognize one's emotions and thoughts and their influence on behavior	**Self-management:** The ability to regulate one's emotions, thoughts, and behaviors effectively in different situations	**Social awareness:** The ability to take the perspective of and empathize with others	**Relationship skills:** The ability to establish and maintain healthy and rewarding relationships with diverse individuals and groups
Schema connections	*Aggregating* *Connecting*	*Transforming* *Trajectory*	*Orientation* *Perspective*	*Connecting* *Enclosing*
Social Thinking Methodology connections	Thinking Thoughts and Feeling Feelings	Flexible and Stuck Thinking Size of the Problem	Thinking Thoughts and Feeling Feelings	Sharing an Imagination Hidden Rules and Expected and Unexpected Behaviors

Schema connections	*Aggregating Connecting*	*Transforming Trajectory*	*Orientation Perspective*	*Connecting Enclosing*
"How Does Your Engine Run?" Alert Program connections	Identifying current engine level and the expected engine level for a particular activity or task	Changing from one level of alertness to another (e.g., from fast to medium)	Recognizing the engine level of others as well as of book characters	Identifying appropriate engine level for group activities
Zones of Regulation connections	Introduction to feelings with corresponding zones	Red Zone feelings Yellow Zone feelings	Blue Zone feelings Red Zone feelings	Green Zone feelings
Literature resources	*In My Heart: A Book of Feelings* by Jo Witek *When Sophie Gets Angry—Really, Really Angry . . .* by Molly Bang *It Was Supposed to Be Sunny* by Samantha Cotterill *The Most Magnificent Thing* by Ashley Spires *Fergel Is Fuming!* by Robert Starling	*A Little SPOT of Flexible Thinking* by Diane Alber *Beautiful Oops* by Barney Saltzberg *Ish* by Peter H. Reynolds *Regina's Big Mistake* by Marissa Moss *My Mouth Is a Volcano* by Julia Cook *What Do You Do with a Problem?* by Kobi Yamada *Big Problems, Little Problems* by Ben Feller	*Fill a Bucket* by Carol McCloud *Duck! Rabbit!* by Amy Krouse Rosenthal *We Disagree* by Bethanie Deeney Murguia *Neither* by Airlie Anderson	*All Are Welcome* by Alexandra Penfold *The Creature of Habit* by Jennifer Smith *Maxine and the Greatest Garden Ever!* by Ruth Spiro *We Are Together* by Britta Teckentrup

Appendix G

Play Schemas and Related Children's Literature

Aggregating

Mushroom in the Rain by Mirra Ginsburg

The Mitten by Jan Brett

The Big Umbrella by Amy June Bates

Be Kind by Pat Zietlow Miller

The Diggers by Margaret Wise Brown

Brick by Brick by Heidi Woodward Sheffield

Connecting/Disconnecting

Whose Bones Are Those? by Chihiro Takeuchi

Some Things Go Together by Charlotte Zolotow

Rosa's Big Bridge Experiment by Jessica Spanyol

Grandma Lena's Big Ol' Turnip by Denia Lewis Hester

Enclosing/Enveloping

Dear Juno by Soyung Pak

A Dress with Pockets by Lily Murray

Katy No Pocket by Emmy Payne

In a Jar by Deborah Marcero

Memory Jars by Vera Brosgol

Orientation/Perspective

The Artist Who Painted a Blue Horse by Eric Carle

To Live on an Island by Emma Bland Smith

The Game of Light by Hervé Tullet

Round Trip by Ann Jonas

Duck! Rabbit! by Amy Krouse Rosenthal

The Upside-Down Fish by Kate Louise

Good News, Bad News by Jeff Mack

I Am Eyes, Ni Macho by Leila Ward

This Is How We Do It by Matt Lemothe

What If You Had . . . book series by Sandra Markle

And They All Saw a Cat by Brendan Wenzel

Zoom by Istvan Banyai

Noticing by Kobi Yamada

Rotation/Circularity

Circle by Jeannie Baker

Meet Mimi by Francie Doland

The Tortilla Factory by Gary Paulsen

Lots of Dots by Craig Frazier

What Do Wheels Do All Day? by April Jones Prince

The Very Busy Spider by Eric Carle

Trajectory

Motion: Push and Pull, Fast and Slow by Darlene Stille

And Everyone Shouted, "Pull!" A First Look at Forces and Motion by Claire Llewellyn

Discover Fireworks by Calee M. Lee

Pezzettino by Leo Lionni

The Red Carpet by Rex Parkin

Go! Go! Go! Stop! by Charise Mericle Harper

Transforming

Magic Trash: A Story of Tyree Guyton and His Art by J. H. Shapiro

The Bluest of Blues: Anna Atkins and the First Book of Photographs by Fiona Robinson

Hiding In . . . book series by Deborah Underwood

Martin's Big Words by Doreen Rappaport

Malala's Magic Pencil by Malala Yousafzai

Greta and the Giants by Zoë Tucker

What If . . . by Samantha Berger

Magic by Mirelle Ortega

The Important Book by Margaret Wise Brown

Dragon Soup by Michael Yu

Idea Jar by Adam Lehrhaupt

Pool by Jihyeon Lee

What Do You Do with an Idea? by Kobi Yamada

What Do You Do with a Chance? by Kobi Yamada

What Do You Do with a Problem? by Kobi Yamada

Trying by Kobi Yamada

Noticing by Kobi Yamada

Maybe by Kobi Yamada

Inside My Imagination by Marta Arteaga

I See by R. Henderson

What Matters by Alison Hughes

Apart, Together: A Book about Transformation by Linda Booth Sweeney

Transporting

1, 2, 3 to the Zoo by Eric Carle

How Does It Move? by Bobbie Kalman

Food Trucks! by Jeffrey Burton

Handa's Surprise by Eileen Browne

References

Compton, Michelle Kay, and Robin Chappele Thompson. 2020. *Makerspaces: Remaking Your Play and STEAM Early Learning Areas*. St. Paul, MN: Redleaf Press.

Curtis, Deb, and Nadia Jaboneta. 2019. *Children's Lively Minds: Schema Theory Made Visible*. St. Paul, MN: Redleaf Press.

Edwards, Carolyn, Lella Gandini, and George Forman. 2012. *The Hundred Languages of Children*. Santa Barbara, CA: Praeger.

Einstein, Albert. 1931. *Cosmic Religion and Other Opinions and Aphorisms*. Cited in Ethan Siegel. "Einstein's Most Famous Quote Is Totally Misunderstood." Big Think. April 11, 2023. https://bigthink.com/starts-with-a-bang/einstein-famous-quote-misunderstood.

Harvard Graduate School of Education Project Zero. 2022. "See, Think, Wonder." https://pz.harvard.edu/sites/default/files/See%20Think%20Wonder_3.pdf.

Haughey, Sally. 2021. "A Call to DEFEND THE WONDER!" Fairy Dust Teaching (email correspondence, March 14).

Jana, Laura A. 2018. "Skills Every Child Will Need to Succeed in 21st Century." Filmed March 28. TEDx Talk, 7:47. www.ted.com/talks/dr_laura_a_jana_skills_every_child_will_need_to_succeed_in_21st_century.

Nutbrown, Cathy. 2011. *Threads of Thinking: Schemas and Young Children's Learning*. 4th ed. London: Sage Publications.

Ralphs, Alexis. 2023. "A Guide to Schema Play in Toddlers." One Hundred Toys. August 21. www.onehundredtoys.com/understanding-schema-play-in-toddlers.

Saltzberg, Barney. 2010. *Beautiful Oops*. New York: Workman.

Stacey, Susan. 2011. *The Unscripted Classroom: Emergent Curriculum in Action.* St. Paul, MN: Redleaf Press.

———. 2018. *Emergent Curriculum in Early Childhood Settings: From Theory to Practice.* St. Paul, MN: Redleaf Press.

———. 2023. *Pedagogical Documentation in Early Childhood: Sharing Children's Learning and Teachers' Thinking.* St. Paul: Redleaf Press.

Vecchi, Vea. 2010. *Art and Creativity in Reggio Emilia: Exploring the Role and Potential of Ateliers in Early Childhood Education.* New York: Routledge.

Vygotsky (Vygotskij), Lev S. (1976). Immaginazione e Creatività Infantile. Roma: Editori Riuniti. Cited in Federico Manzi, Giulia Savarese, Monica Mollo, and Antonio Iannaccone. "Objects as Communicative Mediators in Children with Autism Spectrum Disorder." National Center for Biotechnology Information. June 17, 2020. https://www.ncbi.nlm.nih.gov/pmc/articles/PMC7311758/#B67.

Index

A

B

C

D

T

U

V

W

Z

About Our Schools

National Child Research Center

www.ncrcpreschool.org

As the oldest continuously operating preschool in the District of Columbia, we are proud to continue to provide children with an experience that lasts a lifetime. National Child Research Center nurtures the whole child—socially, emotionally, and intellectually—toward a lifelong love of learning. Informed by current research and continuing education, NCRC's exceptional faculty guide each student's unique development through a play-based, emergent curriculum in a diverse, family-focused community, with a commitment to the inclusion of children who benefit from additional supports and adaptations.

At the heart of NCRC, we value collaboration, learning from one another, and sharing ideas, traditions, and talents in a diverse and inclusive community. Children explore, create, and experience the wonder of play to discover their view of the world around them.

Our child-centered program is a play-based curriculum rooted in sound research and developmentally appropriate practices that reveal and enhance each child's skills through endless opportunities. Every child belongs because each child brings added gifts to the community.

The Sunflower School

https://thesunflowerschool.ca

The Sunflower School is a full-time child care and early childhood education center providing care for children aged one year old to four years old, and before- and after-school programs for children four years old to ten years old in three buildings. The teachers at the Sunflower School work in the Reggio-inspired practice with over fifteen years of experience. Our forty educators train and practice in this approach with the guidance and support of the executive director, Heather Jackson. Our children and educators explore the natural world around our schools with many journeys to the forest and marshlands. The magical, beautiful work of our children can be seen on Instagram @thesunflowerschool and @thesunflower_studio and @tsplaystudio.

The schools are located in the small town of Orangeville, Ontario, Canada.